CONFLICT OF LAWS

I. CONTEXT OF CHOICE OF LAW/CONFLICT OF LAW PROBLEMS

A. HISTORICAL CONTEXT

Historically, most disputes were "local" in the sense that the entire incident or dispute took place within a single jurisdiction—the same country or state. In those situations, there was no question as to which law applied. The case would be brought in the local court, and local law would be applied. Nonetheless, there were still occasions (such as those arising from trade and commerce) in which more than one jurisdiction could claim that its laws should apply. With the increasing integration and internationalization of trade, travel, and even the most mundane transactions, the frequency and complexity of multi-jurisdiction issues has increased. In those cases, there may be a problem in determining which law applies.

B. DEFINITION OF CHOICE OF LAW

On increasingly rare occasions there may still be unclear issues of choice of law. When more than one set of laws could apply to a transaction or event, either because one or more of the events occured outside of the forum state or one or more of the parties does not reside in the forum state, the decisionmaker will face a "choice of law" problem, that is, deciding which forum's law will apply. This choice can be between different states or different countries.

C. PROOF OF LAW

One of the basic elements of any choice of law problem is proof of the relevant foreign law. In interstate disputes, courts are generally willing to take judicial notice of another state's law. Courts are also willing to take judicial notice of treaties that the United States has ratified. As a practical matter, of course, a court in one jurisdiction may not have access to the state law in another jurisdiction, but no particular form of proof is required. When it comes to foreign laws, however, various courts have different processes. In federal court, there is a specific provision for the proof of foreign *statutory* law. Proof of *non-statutory* foreign laws is often done through expert testimony if agreement on the substance of the law cannot be made by counsel.

II. GENERAL CONSIDERATION

A. FEDERAL/STATE

In some cases, there are both state and federal laws that might apply to a particular dispute. This is known as "concurrent jurisdiction." Whether the case is filed in state or federal court, the judge must still determine which law will apply. Simply because an action is filed in federal court does not mean that federal law will apply or even be preferred.

1. **Federal Rights or Causes of Action—Supremacy**

   Because of the "Supremacy Clause" in Article VI of the Constitution, states do not have the power to intrude on federal matters. For example, states may not legislate on patent law issues (federal matter) nor may they conduct their own foreign policy. As such, when a cause of action or defense arises under federal law—the Constitution, federal law, admiralty, or under an applicable federal court order—federal law will apply to the exclusion of any state law regardless of whether the action is filed in federal court or state court.

2. **Conflicts between Federal and State Law—Preemption**

   There are some areas that are not necessarily federal but which Congress has chosen to exercise its power to control. To the extent it is determined that Congress has intended to control the field to the exclusion of state law, then the federal law is deemed to have "preempted" the state law. For example, in the area of pension rights, the ERISA law is deemed to control in all areas in which it applies, and state law is disregarded. On the other hand, while there are a variety of federal laws concerning the environment, there are many aspects that are also subject to state law.

3. **State Rights or Causes of Action—Where No Federal Right Is Asserted**

   In general, state law may still apply to state rights or causes of action regardless of what court is considering the case. This may arise in federal court in one of two ways. First, the federal case may involve other federal claims that give the federal court jurisdiction. Second, the case may be brought as a diversity case between parties of different states. In either event, ever since the Supreme Court's decision in *Erie Railroad v. Tompkins*, 304 U.S. 64 (1938), federal courts apply state substantive law to state causes of action. Under *Erie*, federal courts still apply federal procedure to cases before them. However, if the suit is filed in federal court, federal procedural rules will be applied. (The substantive/procedural distinction is discussed in § II C below.)

B. INTERNATIONAL CASES

1. **Special Considerations**

   In addition to other choice of law issues, there are several matters that apply only to conflicts between the laws of different countries. Among them are the effect of treaties, the impact of special, country-specific legislation, and the interaction with other decisions in the case such as the denial of a motion to dismiss based on *forum non conveniens*.

2. **Treaties**

The Constitution provides that foreign treaties ratified by the United States Senate are to be deemed "the law of the land." Accordingly, to the extent that a treaty contains a specific choice of law determination this must be applied. It is also possible that a cause of action could arise directly under such a treaty, although that is not a frequent occurrence.

3. **Country-Specific Legislation**

As a result of various diplomatic decisions by the Congress, there are pieces of legislation that are not of general application but apply only to one or a few countries. The effect of such legislation may be to modify, or even eliminate, state causes of action.

4. **Interaction with Other Court Actions**

Because transnational cases raise a plethora of procedural and substantive issues, courts may be faced with other decisions that may affect its choice of law. For example, they may be reluctant to dismiss a case on jurisdictional or venue grounds but then be concerned that retention of jurisdiction could lead to or be perceived as forum shopping. In those cases, the court may be more inclined to apply the foreign jurisdiction's law than otherwise.

C. SUBSTANCE V. PROCEDURE

1. **Nature of Issue**

In either the state/federal or interstate choice of law context, the courts are generally deciding which substantive law to apply but will still apply their own procedures or the procedural law of the forum state to the case. Although the general principle is easy to state, its application can be exceptionally murky.

2. **Substantive—Impact on Outcome**

A substantive rule of law is one that may materially affect the outcome of the case, at least as it relates to a particular cause of action. If the suit is filed in federal court, then the court will apply federal law to resolve the substance and procedure dichotomy.

3. **Procedural—Rules of Operation**

Rules that merely govern the mechanics of the litigation are procedural in nature. Nonetheless, it must be observed that in particular situations, almost any procedural rule could affect who wins or loses the case. For example, if the plaintiff fails to serve a defendant properly and thereby misses a statute of limitations, dismissal on "procedural" grounds would, in effect, dispose of the case.

4. **Specific Examples**

a. **Mechanics of Instituting and Conducting Litigation.** In general, the mechanical rules of starting and conducting a case are considered to be procedural. The forum court is entitled to determine how service is to be accomplished, how pleadings are to be set forth and filed, how parties are to be joined or denominated, and similar matters.

b. **Burden of Proof.** In some cases, the burden of proof is specifically allocated or quantified by the source of substantive law in order to define a substantive outcome. For example, when a statute requires the proponent of a will to prove capacity on the part of the testator, that would be a substantive requirement. On the other hand, mere allocation of the obligation to go forward on a particular issue—that is, who has the initial obligation to introduce evidence on an issue—is procedural.

c. **Presumptions.** As with the burden of proof, if the presumption simply determines who must first raise an issue or introduce evidence, then it is procedural. For example, the presumption of regularity simply means that the person seeking to challenge regularity must start rather than the person seeking to establish such regularity. In contrast, a presumption that has evidentiary weight or that is irrebuttable would be substantive.

d. **Rules Governing the Introduction of Evidence.** Typically, rules of evidence are procedural because they relate to the methods by which evidence is introduced rather than the outcome of the dispute.

e. **Privilege.** Although privilege is often considered to be an evidentiary issue, it may be treated differently because the foundation for granting privilege may arise in another jurisdiction that has a policy embodied in that privilege. For example, the policy underlying the marital privilege is usually seen as having more to do with the regulation of the marital relationship than it does with evidence. As a result, courts will often look to the state that has the most significant relationship to the communication that is at issue to decide which rule relating to privilege will apply.

f. **Statutes of Limitation.** Although seemingly dispositive, statutes of limitation describe what actions the forum court will permit to be brought before it. As a result, they have been historically deemed to be procedural. That approach, however, has changed in many states to a more flexible approach that seeks to identify the jurisdiction that has the most significant relationship to the underlying claim to decide which statute of limitations will apply.

g. **Contract Formation Rules.** Although often framed as procedural, the requisites for the formation and interpretation of a contract are, in fact, substantive in nature. For example, the Statute of Frauds is considered to be substantive.

D. IMPACT OF POLICY

Cutting across all choice of law problems is the fundamental notion that a forum need not apply law that it finds to be repugnant to the policies of the jurisdiction in which it sits. Thus, courts need not recognize marriages that the forum state deems to be incestuous or improper. Similarly, at least some courts have determined that another state's damages limitations need not be applied because they are so low that they are inappropriate.

III. COMMON CONFLICTS PROBLEMS

A. "RENVOI"

Not every state or country has the same set of choice of law rules. As a result, there can be situations when the choice of law of the first forum refers a decision to the laws of a second forum whose choice of law rules indicate either that the first forum's laws or the laws of a third jurisdiction entirely should decide the matter. *NOTE: This problem only arises if the first forum applies the ENTIRE body of the second forum's law rather than the substantive rules of decision.*

1. Transmission/Remission

In the jargon of conflict of laws, *"transmission"* occurs when the second forum's laws require the application of a third forum's laws. *"Remission"* occurs when the second forum's choice of law rules sends the dispute back to the first jurisdiction's laws.

2. Responses to Renvoi

The majority response to renvoi is simply to ignore it and apply only the substantive decisional law of the second forum. Both Restatements essentially adopt this position, and it is consistent with the modern approach, which de-emphasizes technical rules and focuses on policy. A second approach is for the first forum's court (or arbitrator) to put itself in the place of the second forum's courts and determine how that court would decide the matter—which could require the application of the policy approach. Other approaches would apply renvoi but cut it off after the first transmission or remission, or to formally trace the decisions by rule until a final substantive law can be applied.

B. DEPEÇAGE

Under the modern approach, the court resolves all choice-of-law issues on an adhoc or issue-by-issue basis. The historical approach is to analyze the case as in its entirety.

C. FALSE CONFLICT

Before engaging in a complex, choice of law analysis, courts will often check the relevant forums' laws to determine if there is any meaningful difference. When there is no such difference, a "false" conflict of law is presented because there is no real conflict. In such circumstances, the practical (and common) approach is to determine that the laws are substantially similar and decline to go through a formal choice of law analysis. A false conflict also arises when only one state has a legitimate interest in applying its laws.

D. TRUE CONFLICT

If more than one state has a legitimate interest in applying its own laws, there are several approaches to resolving a true conflict: Preference is for using the forum's law if the conflict cannot otherwise be avoided or "comparative impairment" where a federal court will apply the law of the using the doctrine of forum most impaired by the conflict.

E. STATUTORY CHOICE OF LAW

Although most choice of law disputes are resolved by common law rules, there are some statutes that may be dispositive of the conflict of law issues. If the forum state does have such a law in place, that forum's courts will follow the statutory rule.

1. Statutes of Limitations—Borrowing

The majority of states have specific statutes that require the application of the statute of limitations of the state in which the cause of action arose or in which the defendant resides. Such statutes are put in place to avoid forum-shopping by defendants who, for example, try to take advantage of a more "generous" statute in another state.

2. Wills

Because of the policy favoring the validity of wills, many states provide that if a will is contested, the rules concerning the execution of a will are to be those of the state in which the will is executed rather than the state in which the suit is brought. This also serves the interest of predictability, because the location at which a will was executed is easily determined.

3. Federal Tort Claims Act

This statute contains a choice of law provision that mandates the application of the law of the place where the tortious act or omission took place. This is not limited to the substantive law of that location; however, the choice of law rules of that location must also be applied. (In general, however, those choice of law rules will still apply the location of the act or omission.)

F. CONTRACTUAL CHOICE OF LAW

In a variety of other contexts, parties can agree among themselves ahead of time on the law to be applied to a particular situation. Almost all commercial contracts as well as many licenses or other commercial relationships contain a choice of law provision. Assuming that such a clause is enforceable, then such choice will be enforced unless the law bears no meaningful relationship to the dispute in question.

IV. CHOICE OF LAW ANALYSIS

A. OVERVIEW

There are a variety of ways that courts analyze choice of law problems. As a result, there is no single right answer in the abstract. For example, if a specific jurisdiction is at issue, then that particular jurisdiction's approach must be used. If no specific jurisdiction is identified, then each of the major analytical techniques should be considered to identify the possible outcomes.

B. TRADITIONAL ANALYSIS

In the traditional approach, the first step is to define the type of dispute before the court (also called "characterization"). Thus, the court will determine whether the case is a property case or a tort case, for example. Once the court decides the category in which the case fits, it then applies the special rules for that type of case. Accordingly, much turns on the initial abstract classification of the type of dispute.

1. "Vested Rights"

The traditional approach is often called the "vested rights" approach. The concept here is that a cause of action is considered to be a "right" in the sense of a property right, and that at some point it crystallizes ("vests") in the plaintiff. This approach then creates different rules for different types of causes of action—tort, contract, real estate, etc.—because the vesting of the right depends on different types of events. Nonetheless, assuming all states followed this approach, in theory there would be no divergence in the choice of law regardless of the forum in which the suit is brought.

2. Implications of the Traditional Analysis

Jurisdictions that follow the traditional analysis typically use the "whole case" approach that applies one jurisdiction's laws to the entire case rather than selecting law issue-by-issue. *See* § IV B above.

3. **Advantages of the Traditional Analysis**

To the extent that a case can be easily classified, the traditional approach is relatively mechanical and predictable. While it is easy to over-focus on cases on the margin, many cases are, in fact, relatively easy to classify. For example, there is no doubt that a slip-and-fall case is a tort action, and the application of the rule that the law of the place of injury governs is simple and easy to apply.

4. **Disadvantages**

Given the variety of types of causes of action in modern jurisprudence, however, there are increasingly large numbers of cases which do not fit comfortably in any standard category. The clarity of the traditional approach can also be overstated; many commentators have asserted that courts often manipulated the traditional analysis to obtain a particular result. Thus, courts may deem a substantive rule to be procedural, may invoke a public policy to invalidate the other state's law, or may use some other device to evade the application of a law that it believes to be inequitable.

C. MODERN ANALYSIS—MOST SIGNIFICANT RELATIONSHIP

Rejecting the rigidity of the traditional analysis, the modern approach attempts to determine what law is most relevant to each issue presented by the case. In theory, without sacrificing the general objective of uniform application of law, the modern approach focuses on a potpourri of factors to identify the law that bears the most significant relationship to a particular issue.

1. **Factors to Be Considered**

    a. **Needs of Interstate/International Commerce.** In light of the increasing integration and interdependence of jurisdictions, the court should consider which rule is best to facilitate interstate/international commerce.

    b. **Certainty and Predictability.** As with the traditional analysis, there is a substantial value in ensuring a consistent result regardless of which forum has the dispute. Thus, while no longer the sole consideration, it is still an important factor.

    c. **Policies of the Forum.** One of the factors the court must consider is the policy interest of the forum in which it sits. If the purposes of that policy will be served by applying the forum law, that will militate in favor of the forum state's law.

    d. **Policies of Non-Forum States.** The forum state must also consider the policies of all other states that might have an interest in the application of their laws.

e. **Policies Inherent in the Issue in Question.** Taking the case issue by issue, there are some general tendencies in each field that must also be taken into account. For example, there is a general policy in favor of the validity of a will. The court should consider which law will be consistent with that overall intention.

f. **Expectations of the Parties.** In some fields of law, the parties form reasonable expectations as to which law will apply. Thus, in contract, property, family law, and trusts and estates, to name a few, those involved in the transaction may have acted on the belief that a particular law will apply, and this should be considered by the forum court.

g. **Convenience.** In close decisions, the court may also take into account its own convenience in determining or applying the relevant law. This is particularly true when the differences in the possible laws are relatively minor. See discussion of False Conflicts in § II C above.

h. **Party's Domicile.** The party's domicile generally is the most significant relationship, particularly where the domicile is the forum state.

2. **Specific Types of Cases**

In addition to the foregoing general principles, there are often certain specific contacts that are given credence in substantive contexts. These are embodied in the Second Restatement.

3. **Advantages**

The advantage of the modern approach is that it is more flexible than the former rules-based approach. Thus, it depends less on the initial categorization of the case and more on the specifics of each case. It is also more likely to serve real policy interests rather than the presumed interests implicit in the rules.

4. **Disadvantages**

The multiplicity of factors and the judgment required to apply them makes consistency much less likely in the application. Because consistency is one of the purposes of choice of law, the modern approach is much more likely to result in strategic forum shopping.

D. OTHER APPROACHES—GOVERNMENTAL INTERESTS

Another way of framing out a more modern analysis is to focus primarily on the underlying government interests in which law applies. This analysis, therefore, compares the explicit or implicit policies behind the laws involved. (The major proponent of this approach is Professor Brainerd Currie.)

1. **Analytical Process**

   Conceptually, it is easy to apply this analysis. First, the court identifies the possible states that could have interests in having their law apply. Second, it evaluates the strength of the policies, starting with the forum state. Third, if more than one state has an important policy interest, the court must balance the comparative strength of the interests.

2. **False Conflicts in the Governmental Interests Context**

   As noted above, one type of false conflict arises when the laws of the two competing states are not acttually inconsistent, even though they might seem to be at first review. In the context of this analysis, a false conflict can also arise when the laws appear to conflict, but one of the two states, in fact, has no meaningful policy interest in having its law apply.

3. **Resolving Conflicts**

   When there are real conflicts, it is not always clear how the court can balance conflicting interests. One way is to give a presumption in favor of the forum state (the suggestion of the proponent of this analysis).

4. **Advantages**

   The advantage of this approach is that it focuses on the core values that underlie the resolution of any conflict. Thus, rather than applying mechanical rules or multiple factors, it concentrates on the core values at stake.

5. **Disadvantages**

   The central problem with this analysis is that it often gives the court very little practical guidance. When laws are truly in conflict, it is very difficult to weigh or compare two different state's policies. As a result, the outcome will vary greatly on the particular judgment of any given trier of fact.

E. **OTHER APPROACHES—MISCELLANEOUS**

1. **Other Approaches—Similar to Governmental Interests**

   There are a number of variations on the governmental interests analysis that vary only in the way they resolve true conflicts. For example, in an analysis formulated by Harvard professor Arthur von Mehren, the forum court must attempt to dissect and articulate the competing policies to determine which is the "predominantly concerned jurisdiction," that is, which one either has the single strongest concern or which has the most aggregate concerns. If no state predominates, the forum court must look to the strength of the enforcement of

KAPLAN) *pmbr*

the competing laws. Others formulate the analysis differently but come to much the same result.

2. Other Approaches—Principles of Preference

A somewhat different analysis had been proposed by the late Professor David F. Cavers who assigns significant value to the functioning of the federal/multistate system. Under this analysis, the forum court seeks to identify the best rule that would further the relevant states' laws and also serve the principle of fairness. Thus, if one state creates special protections in certain tort cases – such as a "Good Samaritan law" – that law should control even if a citizen from another state is injured and sues in his state's court.

3. Other Approaches—Better Law

Yet another analysis rejects entirely any rules-based approach and instead suggests five criteria to select the better law to apply. Under this analysis, in identifying the better law, the forum court should consider

- Predictability of results
- International and interstate coordination
- Simplification of the judicial task
- The forum's general governmental interests
- The most reasonable and sensible law

V. SPECIFIC AREAS OF LAW

A. OVERVIEW

Under many, if not most, approaches, different rules apply depending on the substantive area of law. This is, of course, most important under the traditional approach for which the type of law can be dispositive. Even under more flexible analyses, however, the courts will take into account the types of law involved.

B. CONTRACT

1. Traditional Rule

The traditional analysis focused on the place in which the contract was made. This led to many hypotheticals about parties signing contracts in a plane flying over multiple jurisdictions. Fortunately, this rule is no longer in general use.

2. Modern Analysis

As a starting point, the modern analysis will give credence to the parties' choice of law unless it bears no meaningful relationship to the contract. Since almost all contracts contain a choice of law provision, this approach resolves almost all contract choice of law issues. In the absence of such an agreed-on provision, however, the court will look to the forum with the most significant relationship to the contract. Thus, the courts will look at the "center of gravity" of the contract, looking not only at the place of contracting but also at the location of the negotiations, the place of performance, the residence of the parties, and the subject matter of the contract.

3. Specific Contract Issues—Contracts of Adhesion

Because courts are very hostile to contracts of adhesion – where one party has substantially less negotiating power than the other – they will look for every reason to avoid a choice of law provision that is in any way unfair. Often the public policy exception is invoked if no other technique will work.

4. Specific Contract Issues—Capacity

The traditional analysis would, as set forth above, focus on the place of making of the contract. The more modern analysis treats capacity as a matter that the forum state has much more interest in than any other state, which would generally result in an application of the forum state's rules.

5. Specific Contract Issues—Illegality

Much of the choice of law when the contract is alleged to be illegal depends on whether the alleged violation is technical or substantive in nature. For technical problems, the courts will tend to try to uphold the validity of the contract if any of the potentially relevant states would permit the contract. This does lead to companies moving to those localities that are favorable to their contracts to take advantage of this rule. On the other hand, when the court determines a meaningful public policy of the forum state is involved, or it believes that the enforcing party was not acting in good faith, it is much more likely to apply the forum law to invalidate the contract.

6. Specific Contract Issues—Statute of Frauds

The traditional analysis depended on the procedural/substantive distinction. If the aspect of the statute that may be applied is deemed to be procedural, then only the forum state's law will apply. The modern analysis rejects that analysis and uses a standard "most substantial interest" analysis.

7. **Specific Contract Issues—Insurance**

The traditional analysis treats insurance contracts like any other type of contract. The more modern approach holds that insurance contracts should be deemed contracts of adhesion and looks to the place of the risk—that is, where the insured property or person is located. Whether a victim has a right of "direct action" (the ability to sue the insurance company directly) is generally construed to be procedural in nature and thus governed by the forum state.

8. **Specific Contract Issues—Negotiable Instruments**

For almost all aspects of a negotiable instrument, the court looks either to the place of creation of the instrument or the place it came to be located. On the other hand, if the dispute concerns the nature of the performance due under the instrument, the courts will look to the place where performance was to take place.

C. PROPERTY

1. **Traditional Analysis**

The traditional analysis began by focusing on the distinction between land and things connected to land ("immovables") and all other property ("movables"). For those things that were part of the land, including leases, rents, proceeds of sales, and improvements to the land, the traditional rule applied the law of the locus of the land. It is worth noting that the traditional rule would apply the "whole law" to the dispute: i.e., the law of the locus of the land including its choice of law rules. As a practical matter, those rules would generally not create a renvoi problem. As to movables, the location of the movable at the time of the dispute was important but could be affected by the nature of the dispute. Thus, if the dispute relates to the inheritance of movables, the law of the deceased owner's domicile at the time of death could control.

2. **Modern Analysis**

In this area, the modern analysis does not differ that much from the traditional. For immovables, the result is almost invariably the same, because the locus of the real estate will have an overwhelming interest in which law applies, and no other state will have much, if any, interest. The only possible exception may come from contracts that relate to the land but which have some independent existence. Thus, a note secured by land—but probably not the mortgage or deed of trust—or a contract to sell land may be treated under contract rules. This does not mean that the outcome will necessarily be different; the locus state will still have a strong interest that must be evaluated, but the analytical process may be different and the outcome in some situations may vary. For movables, the analysis will focus on the most significant relationship to the subject at issue. It should be noted that there will often be a "false conflict," *see* § II C, *supra*, because these disputes are generally covered by the Uniform Commercial Code, which has been adopted in every state.

3. **Property—Secured Interests**

This issue frequently presents a false conflict because the Uniform Commercial Code governs, and the provisions of almost every state are consistent in this respect. As a result, the best analysis is to verify that no real conflict exists and then obviate further analysis.

4. **Property—Intangibles**

When an intangible property right is embodied in a document, the modern analysis begins with that document and its locus. It is conceivable that another jurisdiction could have more interest in the dispute if the document is part of a complex transaction which largely took place elsewhere, but that will be a less likely outcome. For intangibles that are not embodied in a document, courts will either look to the law of the place of the transfer, or, if the issue is a debt, to the domicile of the debtor. If, on the other hand, the issue is not truly a property issue but rather one involving the effectiveness of a contract of transfer, then contract rules will be consulted.

5. **Property—Trusts**

Because there is a general policy in support of the validity of trusts and the actions of trustees, courts will go to significant lengths to find law that will validate that policy. Indeed, to the extent that any rule can be defined, it is that the court will choose the law that meets this policy objective.

D. TORTS

1. **Traditional Rule**

The traditional analysis focused on the law of the place of the "wrong." For the purposes of the analysis, the wrong was generally located at the place of the injury. Historically, simple torts occurred in one place and arose from purely local circumstances. As an extension of this concept to accommodate modern commerce, courts began to identify the place of the wrong as the place of the conduct that led to the injury rather than the harm itself.

a. **Advantages.** The advantage of this rule is its simplicity. Further, although subject to a variety of practical and theoretical criticisms, on most occasions, this rule satisfies all the needs of the forum court.

b. **Disadvantages.** Many commentators have criticized this rule because they assert that it leads to idiosyncratic and often impractical results. Thus, if two residents of the forum state are involved in litigation in the forum state about an accident between the two of them that just happened to be across the border in another state, that other state's law that would apply. Because the rule is relatively mechanical, it does not take into account the relative weight of any state's policy. Finally, as interstate commerce developed, the place of injury became much less important compared to the location of the negligence.

c. **Development of the Traditional Rule.** As noted above, one way that courts evaded the mechanical application of this rule was to recharacterize the rule as procedural rather than substantive. Another way that courts avoided a result that they did not want was to recategorize the problem so it did not fall into the tort category. As a result, matters of privilege that might be called rules of tort were often categorized as rules of family law. Yet another way that courts evaded the rule was to invoke a doctrine of public policy.

2. **Modern Analysis**

In applying the modern analysis that focuses on the most significant relationship to the tort, the court will look at several factors:

- The place of injury
- The place of the negligent conduct
- The residence of the parties
- The nature of the relationship of the parties

As can be seen from this list, the traditional analysis is not totally rejected because the place of the injury and the location of the conduct are still given substantial weight. Nonetheless, not only are other factors considered, but the relative weight assigned to each factor can change.

a. **Advantages.** As discussed above, this analysis avoids purely mechanical rule application that avoids obviously absurd results. It permits courts to focus on specific situations rather being forced to rely on sweeping generalizations.

b. **Disadvantages.** Because judgment is involved, the modern approach—and its variant, the governmental interest analysis—is much more likely to produce non-uniform results. In the tort context (in which the victim has little meaningful ability to create in advance a choice of law rule) this poses a substantial ex post facto problem.

c. **Specific Torts—Product Liability.** As noted above, even under the traditional analysis, courts shifted the focus of the place of the wrong from the place of injury to the place of the negligent conduct. The modern approach, although phrasing its results in various ways, recognizes that the happenstance of the place of injury often has little relevance. As a result, the focus tends to be on the domicile of the injured party with some attention given to the place in which the alleged negligence took place. Some commentators have observed that the functional outcome is to find the law that favors the plaintiff.

d. **Specific Torts—Defamation.** Because defamation is a tort that has developed later than traditional torts, it has not received uniform treatment with respect to choice of law issues. Some courts look to the place of publication either as a matter of common law or under the Uniform Single Publication Act. Other courts look either to the place of injury—that is, the law of each state in which the injury occurs—or to the place of conduct.

E. CORPORATE/BUSINESS ORGANIZATIONS

1. Traditional Analysis

The traditional analysis focused on the place of incorporation of the company for all matters of internal operation of such company.

2. Modern Analysis

The modern analysis is very similar to the traditional analysis. Because the state of incorporation is generally considered to have the most significant relationship to a company's internal operations, the outcome will generally be the same. Thus, the powers of a corporation, its ability to sue and be sued, the powers of shareholders and the board of directors, and similar matters are seen as a part of the internal operation of the company. The only exceptions that are generally created are creatures of arguments of the forum state's public policy.

3. Corporations—Federal Law

In considering the applicable law, the supremacy of federal law must be recognized. Thus, if the securities laws or the Sarbanes-Oxley Act contains provisions that are mandatory on the corporation, that law must be enforced.

4. Corporations—Delaware Law

Because so many corporations are incorporated in Delaware, that state has the most articulated body of corporate law of any state. Accordingly, other states will give substantial weight to the analysis of that state's common law. Thus, while not dispositive, reference to Delaware law to "fill in spaces" in another state's law is often the course taken by almost every court.

F. FAMILY LAW

1. Traditional Analysis

For most matters, the traditional analysis is relatively straightforward. The law that applies to marriage is that of the jurisdiction where the marriage took place; the law that applies to divorce is the locus of the divorce; and the law of legitimacy is the law of the underlying marriage.

2. Modern Analysis

The modern analysis does not differ significantly from the traditional analysis.

3. Role of Public Policy

In family law, more important than the distinction between the traditional and modern approaches is the impact of public policy. Marriages that are void as a matter of public policy will not be recognized. This problem has arisen with polygamous, same-sex, or incestuous marriages. In addition, most states no longer permit the distinction of legitimacy to have any legal consequences.

4. Family Law—Adoption

Adoption does not create a choice of law problem because adoption is a creature of statute. Thus, whichever law is used will govern the validity of the adoption.

TRUE-FALSE QUESTION
TOPIC LIST

1. Choice of law/domicile

2. Citizenship/domicile/residence

3. Domicile/physical presence

4. Domicile/intent

5. Full Faith and Credit

6. Comity/reciprocity

7. Full Faith and Credit

8. Jurisdiction

9. Correct choice of law standard to apply

10. Differences between choice of law approaches

11. Vested rights approach to choice of law problems

12. Vested rights approach to choice of law problems

13. Combination approaches to choice of law problems

14. Most significant contacts approach

15. Better law approach to choice of law problems

16. Better law approach to choice of law problems

17. Interest analysis approach to choice of law problems

18. Second Restatement view on choice of law

19. "Depeçage" approach to choice of law problems

20. "Lex fori" approach to choice of law problems

21. Choice of law provisions in contracts

22. Conflict of laws issues in domestic relations cases

23. Conflict of laws issues in probate cases

24. *Erie* doctrine/substantive issues

25. *Erie* doctrine/procedural issues

For each question below, circle "T" (true) or "F" (false).

1. **T F** When a plaintiff brings a lawsuit in a state where she is domiciled, there is still a question as to which law to apply.

2. **T F** A person's citizenship is the same thing as his domicile, which is the same thing as his residence.

3. **T F** In order to declare a place to be his domicile, a person must be physically present there.

4. **T F** Intent is required to change domicile.

5. **T F** If a forum has previously acted in a matter, a subsequent forum must respect and honor the decision and judgment of the original forum.

6. **T F** Comity and reciprocity are synonymous terms.

7. **T F** Each state in the United States must recognize and honor the judgments of every other state.

8. **T F** Any state with jurisdiction over a matter can choose to apply its own law, even where there is "on point" law from a sister state.

9. **T F** There is a single "choice of law" standard that is correct for every legal dispute that could involve more than one set of laws.

10. **T F** Even if two states purport to employ the same "choice of law" approach, that approach may actually be quite different in practice.

11. **T F** Under the "vested rights approach," the first step in choosing which law to use is to characterize the cause of action.

12. **T F** Courts are quite dispassionate when applying a vested rights approach.

13. **T F** Some jurisdictions use the vested rights approach for some types of cases but prefer another choice of law approach for others.

14. **T F** The "most significant contacts" approach to choice of law is inherently more flexible than a vested rights approach.

15. **T F** Under the "better law" approach, a judge exposes biases up front.

16. **T F** Under the "better law" approach, a judge may choose the law of whichever state she desires.

17. **T F** A "false conflict" is one where only one state has a true interest in the case and, therefore, in having its law chosen and applied.

18. **T F** The Second Restatement prefers the vested rights approach to choice of law.

19. **T** **F** Under a "depeçage" approach, a court may apply substantive law from more than one state.

20. **T** **F** Some states openly admit that they will always apply their own law when feasible.

21. **T** **F** A choice of law provision in a contract will usually be enforced.

22. **T** **F** In most domestic relations cases, the courts choose the law of the state where the parties are domiciled.

23. **T** **F** In most probate cases, the court chooses to apply the law of the decedent's domicile at the time of his death.

24. **T** **F** In diversity cases, the law of the state in which the federal court sits usually applies.

25. **T** **F** In diversity cases, the Federal Rules of Civil Procedure apply.

ANSWERS TO TRUE-FALSE QUESTIONS

1. False

When a plaintiff brings a lawsuit in a state where she is domiciled, the law of the domicile controls.

2. False

Although a person may live in a different state or country, his citizenship may remain elsewhere. Furthermore, while a person may have several homes, or "residences," for domiciliary purposes, he will have to choose a primary one.

3. True

Under the majority rule, the physical presence can be quite brief. However, a person must actually achieve physical presence to establish a domicile. Mere intent to get to a place where one never arrives does not suffice.

4. True

Physical presence alone does not suffice. It must be accompanied by intent. Generally, intent can be established independently through a person's words or a person's conduct. Therefore, even though a person states that she does not intend to change domiciles, if she lives exclusively in another place, her conduct may be enough to change her domicile.

5. False

For example, if the original forum lacked jurisdiction to hear the case, the subsequent forum need not recognize the decision of that original forum.

6. Somewhat true

(. . . a nice law school answer!) "Comity" refers to the recognition by a domestic court of the decision by a foreign court. Comity usually occurs when a foreign court also agrees to recognize the domestic court's decisions; in other words, comity stems from reciprocity.

7. True

This concept is called the "sister state" doctrine and stems from the Full Faith and Credit Clause of the United States Constitution. Furthermore, federal courts are also bound by the Full Faith and Credit Clause.

8. True

A state may apply its law as long as it has a significant interest in the case and as long as the application is not unfair, arbitrary, or unjust.

9. False

Constitutionally, a court may choose which law to apply under any of several choice of law approaches. These may include, inter alia, an analysis of which law is better or preferable, an interest analysis approach, the Second Restatement approach, a vested rights approach, etc.

10. True

Because states are not required constitutionally to employ any particular approach, and because there is no federal law in place that defines the parameters of a particular choice of law approach, the courts in any state may say that they are employing a certain approach, but may actually be doing so quite differently than another state purporting to use the same approach.

11. True

Under the vested rights approach, there are bright line rules about which law to use. For example, a court might apply different law in a contract action than in a tort action or a will contest. Note that different issues in the cause of action are *not* characterized separately; rather, the overall or predominant characterization will apply to the entire cause of action.

12. False

While some courts might be dispassionate, others will try to predetermine the likely outcome of a case under the law of each jurisdiction. Then the court might characterize the case differently in order to choose law that will produce a favorable result. Such careful characterization is often referred to as "using an escape device."

13. True

In fact, while most courts use the vested rights approach to choose the correct law for wills and real estate issues, most prefer another approach for contracts and torts problems. This is probably because so many courts use escape devices when characterizing cases, and the vested rights approach is therefore deemed unreliable.

14. True

With flexibility, however, comes a lack of predictability. The advantage to a most significant contacts approach is that it ensures that the law employed derives from a state that has been substantially involved in the case, unlike the vested rights approach, where contact could have been transitory or minimal.

15. True

However, this does not necessarily carry a negative connotation. Because many judges would look at outcome anyway if they used a most significant contacts or vested rights approach, "better law" is not fundamentally different in that respect. The "better law" approach allows a judge to be honest about what law is preferred rather than being pressured to use an escape device or dealing with the often murky issue of which contacts are most significant.

16. False

To choose the law of a state with no contacts whatsoever might even violate the Constitution, even if that law were the "best" law. Therefore, a judge must take care to choose the law of a state that has at least some contact with the controversy.

17. True

On the other hand, a "true conflict" is one in which more than one state is connected to the case and would like to have its laws applied. An "unprovided for case" is one where none of the connected cases has a true interest in which law is chosen.

18. False

In fact, the Second Restatement introduces and incorporates many of the more modern approaches to choice of law, including interest analysis, most significant relationship, and better law. The Second Restatement does not recommend any single approach; rather, it encourages state courts to employ the approach or approaches that work best for them.

19. True

Under a "depeçage" approach, a court may apply the substantive law of one state to one issue in a case and the substantive law of another state to another issue. The Second Restatement allows "depeçage," but not all scholars like the approach; it results in a single case being decided under the laws of several states and therefore in mixed results from a policy standpoint.

20. True

This approach is called "lex fori" and is used by a few states. Under this approach, a court admits that it will always apply its own law as long as the forum is connected to the case. The parties, may, of course, rebut the court's presumption that it will employ its own law, but such an argument would have to be quite compelling.

21. True

As long as the chosen forum is substantially connected to the controversy, most courts will enforce a choice of law provision.

22. True

Because people expect their personal lives to be governed by their own states (and, indeed, many people choose their home states based on the laws there), a court will usually apply the law of the forum where they are domiciled.

23. True

In fact, most probate proceedings actually occur in the state where the decedent was domiciled at death.

24. True

Substantive law is defined as that which is outcome determinative; in other words, it will affect the outcome of a case.

25. Mostly true

Where there is a Federal Rule of Civil Procedure on point, it will govern over a state procedural rule. However, if the federal rules do not speak to a procedural issue, then state procedural rules apply.

MULTIPLE CHOICE QUESTION
TOPIC LIST

1. Domicile

2. Full Faith and Credit

3. Personal jurisdiction

4. Choice of law – vested rights approach

5. Choice of law – various approaches

6. Development of choice of law approaches/doctrine

7. Choice of law – vested rights approach

8. Choice of law clauses

9. Choice of law – "lex fori" approach

10. Choice of law – interest analysis approach

11. Choice of law – interest analysis approach

12. *Erie* – procedural conflicts

13. *Erie* – substantive conflicts

14. Choice of law – interest analysis approach

15. Choice of law – issue splitting

KAPLAN *pmbr*

1. In which of the following situations is domicile most likely to change for the stated individual?

   (A) Angus has lived with his parents in State A for 18 years. After his senior year, he goes away to college in State B. He returns to State A for the summer each year that he is in college, but for four years he resides primarily on campus in State B. His car is registered in State A.

   (B) Jennifer, who has lived all of her life in State X, is convicted of money laundering and is sent to federal prison in State Y. She serves a nine-year sentence and is then released. Upon her release, she returns to State X.

   (C) Jacob has lived in State D for 10 years. However, as a member of the Army Reserves, he is called up for active duty and sent to State C to serve there. He serves in State C for two years.

   (D) Mary Anne, as a single woman, has lived in State G for the past 13 years. She marries a man who is a resident of State H and moves there to be with her husband.

2. In which of the following circumstances would Full Faith and Credit apply?

   (A) An action that is *rem* in nature.
   (B) A purely procedural matter.
   (C) A criminal case.
   (D) An *in personam* action.

CONFLICT OF LAWS

Questions 3–5 refer to the following fact pattern.

Henry Academy is a college preparatory school in State D. Henry educates 500 boys in grades 7-12, about half of whom board at the school. The school has eight dormitories for the boys who board.

Before they may attend Henry, all boys must have a physical examination to establish their good health. Furthermore, before they enroll, both they and their parents must sign a contract that relieves the Academy of all liability for any personal injuries that might occur on campus.

Last year, there was a terrible accident at Henry. John Peterson, a boarding student, was running through a wooded portion of campus during cross country practice. On neighboring land, a hunter was out hunting for deer. He saw a rustle in the trees and, believing that he saw a deer, shot at John. John was killed.

John's parents were inconsolable. After consulting with their attorney, they brought an action against Henry Academy in state court in their home state of State G.

3. Would State G have jurisdiction over the case?

   (A) No, because Henry Academy is located in State D.
   (B) No, because the injury occurred in State D.
   (C) Yes, if Henry Academy regularly recruited students from State G.
   (D) Yes, because of the nature of the injury.

4. Assume for the purposes of this question only that State G has jurisdiction over the case. Under a vested rights approach to choice of law, which law is most likely to apply?

   (A) The law of State G.
   (B) The law of State D.
   (C) Federal law.
   (D) None of the above.

5. Assume for the purposes of this question only that State G has jurisdiction over the case. Assume also that, under the law of State G, waivers such as the one the Petersons signed are unenforceable as a matter of public policy. Under the law of State D, however, such waivers are binding. Under which approach to choice of law are the Petersons most likely to recover?

   (A) Vested rights.
   (B) "Lex fori."
   (C) Interest analysis.
   (D) Most significant relationship.

6. Place the following approaches to choice of law in the chronological order of their development.

    I. Vested rights doctrine
   II. Interest analysis
  III. "Depeçage"

(A) III, II, I
(B) II, I, III
(C) I, II, III
(D) III, I, II

Questions 7–11 refer to the following fact pattern.

Jennifer is an aspiring actress. She lives in State X, but she applies for a job as the "love interest" on a new reality TV show to be filmed in State Y, which is on the other side of the country. As a part of her application, Jennifer signs a contract stating that she understands that, even if she is not chosen for the lead role, the producers of the show may broadcast her audition tape in the previews for the show.

Jennifer is not chosen for the lead role. After she learns that her application has been turned down, she sends the producers of the show a letter rescinding her agreement to allow them to use her reality show audition tape.

Three months later, Jennifer is watching television when she sees an ad for the new reality show. To her horror, she sees her audition tape on the screen. In her tape, she is wearing nothing but two lettuce leaves and a hula skirt.

Jennifer immediately contacts the producers of the show and learns that they never received her letter.

In State X, contract law states that a revocation of an authorization to use someone's image need never be received to be enforceable. However, State Y law states that such a revocation is only enforceable upon receipt and acknowledgement.

Jennifer sues the producers and the television network in State X.

7. Under a vested rights approach to choice of law, which state's law should apply?

   (A) The law of State X, because this is a contract case.
   (B) The law of State X, because that is where Jennifer lives.
   (C) The law of State Y, because the show was produced there.
   (D) The law of State Y, because this is a tort claim.

8. Assume for the purposes of this question only that the contract that Jennifer signed had a choice of law clause which stated that, in all disputes, the law of State Y would apply. Is the clause enforceable?

   (A) Yes, because choice of law clauses are generally enforceable.
   (B) Yes, but only for a contract claim.
   (C) No, because State Y does not have a significant relationship to the controversy.
   (D) No, because choice of law clauses are generally unenforceable.

9. Under a "lex fori" approach to choice of law, which state's law should apply?

   (A) The law of State X, but only if the controversy is characterized as a tort.
   (B) The law of State X, because that is the state in which Jennifer has brought suit.
   (C) The law of State Y, but only if the controversy is characterized as a contract.
   (D) The law of State Y, because that is where the contract was drafted and the preview tape was made.

10. Assume for the purposes of this question only that in State Y contract law states that a revocation of an authorization to use someone's image need never be received to be enforceable. However, State X law states that such a revocation is only enforceable upon receipt and acknowledgement. Under an interest analysis approach, how would this conflict be characterized?

   (A) It is a true conflict.
   (B) There is a false conflict.
   (C) This is an unprovided for case.
   (D) None of the above.

11. Based on your answer to question #10, under an interest analysis approach, which law should apply?

    (A) The law of State X.
    (B) The law of State Y.
    (C) Neither the law of State X nor the law of State Y.
    (D) Both the law of State X and the law of State Y.

12. Under *Erie*, which law should a federal court apply to a *procedural* issue?

    (A) The Federal Rules of Civil Procedure.
    (B) The procedural law of the state in which it sits.
    (C) The procedural law of the non-forum state.
    (D) The federal court should choose which procedural rule is best.

13. Under *Erie*, which law should a federal court apply to a *substantive* issue?

    (A) Federal common law.
    (B) The substantive law of the state in which it sits.
    (C) The substantive law of the party state in which the court does not sit.
    (D) The federal court should choose which substantive law rule is best.

Questions 14 and 15 refer to the following fact pattern.

Jeremy and Jane Sanders have been married for 14 years and are residents and citizens of State Bliss. They have lived in State Bliss for 10 years.

While on vacation in State Rue, Jeremy and Jane went out to dinner. With his dinner, Jeremy had three martinis. Jane drank only water. When it came time to leave the restaurant, Jane told Jeremy that he was too intoxicated to drive, but Jeremy insisted on driving anyway. About two miles from the restaurant, Jeremy hit a tree, giving Jane a concussion and crushing her arm so severely that it had to be amputated.

Jane sued Jeremy in State Rue for the injuries she sustained in the car accident there. State Bliss allows spouses to sue each other. State Rue has spousal immunity in place.

14. Under an interest analysis approach, how should this conflict be characterized?

   (A) This is a true conflict.
   (B) This is a false conflict.
   (C) This is an unprovided for case.
   (D) None of the above.

15. What is the best way to resolve this conflict so that Jane can sue her husband in State Rue?

    (A) Because both the injury and the lawsuit were in State Rue, State Rue's spousal immunity policy should apply.
    (B) Choose the "better law."
    (C) Because both Jane and Jeremy were domiciled in State Bliss, the State Rue court should simply apply State Bliss law to the whole controversy.
    (D) The State Rue court should split the issues and apply State Rue law to the tort issue in the case and apply State Bliss law to the spousal immunity issue.

1. (D)

(A), (B) and (C) are all incorrect because students, prisoners, and military personnel do not generally change their domicile when they are residing other than in their home state. Of course, if they choose to stay in the state where they were residing after they no longer have to do so, then they may manifest intent to change domicile. However, this situation does not present itself in any of the fact patterns here. (D) is correct (even though under modern rules, a married woman may maintain a separate domicile from that of her husband).

2. (D)

Full Faith and Credit generally applies to *in personam* actions, but not to actions *in rem* or *quasi in rem*. (A) is therefore incorrect. Furthermore, the Supreme Court has held that no state may enforce the penal laws or judgments of other states; (C) is therefore incorrect. Finally, while substantive law decisions are entitled to full faith and credit, the same is not true of procedural decisions. (B) is therefore wrong.

3. (C)

Because the injury occurred in State D and Henry Academy is located there, the Petersons will need to find a way to establish that State G can assert personal jurisdiction over the Academy. Under a minimum contacts analysis, if the Petersons can establish that Henry Academy recruited students from State G on a regular basis, they can probably support their contention that Henry has subjected itself to jurisdiction there. (A) and (B) are incorrect because, even though the Academy is in State D and the injury occurred in State D, State G may still have jurisdiction over Henry Academy if the Petersons can establish minimum contacts with the forum, as noted above. (D) is incorrect because the nature of the injury is irrelevant in a personal jurisdiction analysis.

4. (B)

It is difficult to know which law is likely to apply based on the information we have, but the law of State D probably has an edge. Under a vested rights approach, the first step that the court will take is to characterize the cause of action. Here, the court could characterize the controversy as a contract claim (because of the contractual waiver of liability), in which case the law of the state where the contract was made (probably State D) would apply. On the other hand, if the court characterizes the action as a tort/wrongful injury controversy, the law of the place of injury (State D) would apply. (A) is incorrect because, even though the Petersons could argue that they signed the contract in their home state of State G and that therefore the contract was made there, that argument is less likely to prevail. (C) is incorrect because federal law will be irrelevant to this controversy.

5. (B)

Under the "lex fori" approach, State G will apply its own law to the controversy. The Petersons need for State G law to apply because that state's law invalidates the waiver that they signed. (A) is incorrect because, as explained in Answer #4, under a vested rights approach, the court is likely to apply the law of State D. (C) is incorrect because, under interest analysis, while it is true that State G is likely to apply its own law, such a choice of law is not as certain as it would be under "lex fori." (D) is incorrect because, under a most significant relationship approach, State D would probably be deemed to have more significant contacts with the controversy.

6. (C)

Choice of law doctrine really began with the vested rights approach under the First Restatement. Later, under the Second Restatement, interest analysis came into play and gradually gained acceptance. Currently, the Second Restatement encourages the mixing of choice of law approaches, "depeçage."

7. (A) or (D)

The answer to this question will depend on how the court characterizes Jennifer's claim. If the court characterizes her claim as a tort claim, then the law of the place of the injury will apply. This will probably be State X, as that is where Jennifer sees the tape and presumably suffers other damage. On the other hand, if the court views this as a contract claim, then the law of the state where the contract was made (probably State Y) will apply. (B) is incorrect because Jennifer's residency, while applicable under a jurisdictional analysis, probably will not be important in a vested rights analysis. (C) is incorrect unless the court feels that, because the show was produced in State Y, that was the locus of the injury.

8. (A)

Choice of law clauses in contracts are generally enforceable unless the chosen law has no contact with the controversy. (B) and (D) are therefore incorrect. (C) is incorrect because State Y certainly has a significant relationship with the controversy; the show was filmed there, Jennifer entered into a contract with a production company based there, and the preview was presumably broadcast from there.

9. (B)

Under a "lex fori" approach, the law of the forum state applies. (B), (C), and (D), while all relevant considerations under other choice of law approaches, are irrelevant under a "lex fori" approach.

10. (C)

This is an unprovided for case. In an unprovided for case, the law of the defendant's state benefits the plaintiff. Here, State Y's law is far more advantageous for Jennifer, because she could recover under the law of that state but not under the law of her own. (A) is the second best answer, since there is a true conflict here in that both states have an interest in the controversy. (B) is incorrect. A false conflict is a situation where only one of the states has an interest in the controversy.

11. (B)

Although Jennifer is a resident of State X, and a State X court would conceivably like to see her recover for the harm she has suffered, under an interest analysis approach, the State X court will probably apply its own law. This is because, in true conflicts and unprovided for cases, the law of the forum is usually applied. (A), (C), and (D) are therefore incorrect.

12. (A)

Under *Erie*, when a federal court sits in diversity, it should "choose" the Federal Rules of Civil Procedure instead of the conflicting procedural rules of the state in which it sits. Therefore, (B), (C), and (D) are all incorrect.

13. (B)

Under *Erie*, when a federal court sits in diversity, it should "choose" the substantive law of the state in which it sits instead of the conflicting substantive law of any other interested state. (C) and (D) are therefore incorrect. (A) is incorrect because the *Erie* doctrine developed in response to the development of federal common law; *Erie* was intended to *halt* any such development.

14. (B)

This is a great example of a false conflict case. In a false conflict case, the forum state has no real interest in the case because neither party is domiciled in that state and the injury just happened to occur there. In such cases, the law of the interested state (here, State Bliss, where Jane and Jeremy live) will usually apply. (A) is therefore incorrect. (C) is incorrect; an unprovided for case is one in which the law of defendant's state benefits the plaintiff. Here, both plaintiff and defendant are from the same state.

15. (D)

"Issue-splitting" is a commonly used "escape device." In this case, just as in *Haumschild v. Continental Casualty Co.*, 7 Wis. 2d 130 (1959), the real case on which this question is based, the court will want to use the law of the forum state, where the injury occurred, to rule on the tort issue. However, as to the spousal immunity question, the court will probably want to use the law of the state where the parties are domiciled (State Bliss). (A), (B), and (C) are therefore incorrect, as none of these approaches would allow the law of different states to apply to different issues in the controversy. Note that, under the modern view of the Second Restatement, courts often "mix" law, or apply the law of different states to different issues in the controversy.

1. Personal jurisdiction

2. Choice of law – vested rights approach

3. Choice of law – most significant relationship approach

4. Choice of law – better law approach

5. Personal jurisdiction

6. Choice of law – "lex fori" approach

7. Choice of law – interest analysis approach

8. Choice of law – depeçage

9. *Erie* doctrine – procedural issues

10. *Erie* doctrine – substantive issues

Essay questions 1–4 refer to the following fact pattern.

Smith Dolls, Inc. is a doll manufacturing company located and incorporated in State Y. The company manufactures "Little Tracy" dolls, fashion dolls with many small parts. Unfortunately, there have been a number of documented incidents of choking with Little Tracy dolls when small children have put the small parts in their mouths.

In October 2002, Great Toys, a toy store located in State X (a state about 500 miles from State Y), placed an order for 25 Little Tracy dolls. This was Great Toys' fifth such order for Little Tracy dolls in the past year. Smith Dolls shipped the dolls from State Y to Great Toys at the beginning of November. Great Toys immediately sold out of the dolls, as many parents purchased them for their children for holiday gifts.

Sarah Simpson, a two-year-old girl living in State X, received a Little Tracy doll for Christmas. She loved the doll and began carrying it everywhere. Unfortunately, at the beginning of January, Sarah took the doll into her crib with her for a nap. While in her crib, she began chewing on the doll and swallowed a small doll shoe. When her father came into the room a couple of hours later to get her up, he found her dead in her crib. The cause of death was determined to be choking and asphyxiation. The autopsy found the Little Tracy shoe lodged in Sarah's throat had cut off her air supply. No other factors contributed to Sarah's death.

John and Katherine Simpson, Sarah's parents, have sued Smith Dolls for wrongful death and breach of implied warranty in state court in State X. They claim $100,000,000 in damages.

State X and State Y have different ways of measuring damages in wrongful death actions. State Y measures such damages by calculating the amount of pecuniary loss suffered by the plaintiffs. The limit on recovery is $5,000,000. However, State X looks to the negligence and fault of the manufacturer and limits recovery to $100,000.

1. Does State X have jurisdiction to hear the case? Why or why not?

2. Assume for the purposes of this question only that the State X court does have jurisdiction over the case and uses a vested rights approach to choice of law in this case. What law will apply? What are the pros and cons of this approach?

3. Assume for the purposes of this question only that the State X court does have jurisdiction over the case and uses a most significant relationship approach to choice of law in this case. What law will apply? What are the pros and cons of this approach?

4. Assume for the purposes of this question only that the State X court does have jurisdiction over the case and uses a better law approach to choice of law in this case. What law will apply? What are the pros and cons of this approach?

Essay questions 5–8 refer to the following fact pattern.

Jonathan Myers is a collector of vintage cars living in the state of Pistonacre. He particularly likes old Buick and Cadillac convertibles. Looking at an online auction site late one night, he falls in love with a vintage Caddy with a red convertible top and decides to bid on it. He notices that the seller is a used car dealership located and incorporated in the neighboring state of Gasacre.

Jonathan is ecstatic to learn, three days later, that his bid is the winning bid. He flies to Gasacre to pick up the car, paying cash. He signs the sales contract, which relieves the seller of any and all responsibility for any defects to the car, then drives the car home. No sooner does he pull into his driveway the next day, however, than the engine explodes, setting the car on fire, destroying the entire vehicle.

Jonathan sues the used car dealer in Pistonacre for breach of contract and breach of Pistonacre's lemon laws. In his complaint, he maintains that, although the contract disclaimed any responsibility for defects in the car, such a clause was not enforceable under Pistonacre state law and should be severed. Pistonacre's lemon laws state that sellers remain responsible for any safety defects in used cars for 30 days after the sale. Gasacre's lemon laws contain no such provision. Pistonacre's lemon laws state that all used car sales contracts contain an implied 30-day safety warranty and that such warranty need not be express to be enforceable. Gasacre's commercial code states that contracts for the sale of motor vehicles are enforceable as written, and that any warranties must be expressly provided for in the contract.

5. Does the Pistonacre state court have jurisdiction over the case?

6. Assume for the purposes of this question only that the Pistonacre court does have jurisdiction over the case and uses a "lex fori" approach to choice of law in this case. What law will apply? What are the pros and cons of this approach?

7. Is there a true conflict in this case? Why or why not?

8. Assume for the purposes of this question only that the Pistonacre court does have jurisdiction over the case and uses "depeçage" in this case. What law will apply? What are the pros and cons of this approach?

Essay questions 9 and 10 refer to the following fact pattern.

Cain is an individual living in the state of Pastel. Abel, Inc., is a corporation located and incorporated in the state of Watercolor.

Cain purchased a rare painting worth $110,000 from Abel. However, when the painting arrived, it had a rip in the canvas. An art appraiser has written a report stating that the painting is not repairable and as such is relatively worthless. He has suggested that Cain sell the painting at an art sale to take place at the a local hotel. No painting at the sale will cost more than $49.

Cain did not report the damage to the painting to Abel until 4 months and 5 days after he received it. His reason for this delay was that he wanted to get the appraisal done before he reported the defect.

The P.C.C. (Pastel Commercial Code) requires that a buyer report any nonconformities to the seller with 90 days of receipt of the goods. Otherwise, the buyer waives his rights and must pay the contract price. However, the W.C.C. (Watercolor Commercial Code) allows the buyer to report nonconformities within 150 days.

Cain sues Abel in federal district court in the state of Watercolor. In the breach of contract complaint, no amount of monetary damage is specified. The Watercolor Rules of Civil Procedure specify that, for commercial torts, the amount of damage must be set forth in the complaint. Under the Federal Rules of Civil Procedure, it is not required that the amount of damages be specified.

Abel has filed a motion to dismiss claiming that the complaint is defective because it fails to specify the loss.

9. What law should the federal district court apply in deciding the motion to dismiss?

10. Assume for the purposes of this question only that the motion to dismiss is denied. What law should the federal district court apply in deciding the breach of contract claim?

1. Does State X have jurisdiction to hear the case? Why or why not?

Minimum contacts

Under a minimum contacts analysis, State X should have jurisdiction to hear the case.

Doing business in state frequently

First, the facts are clear that Smith Dolls has done business on many occasions with Great Toys in State X. In fact, Smith Dolls has sold at least 125 dolls to Great Toys alone. Although the facts are not clear on whether Smith Dolls has sold dolls to other businesses in State X, because Little Tracy dolls appear to be popular, it is likely that the company has done quite a bit of business in State X. Because a minimum contacts analysis will look at the frequency and amount of business done in the forum state, it is important to note that Smith Dolls has sold a lot of dolls over the past year in State X.

Claim arises out of contacts

A minimum contacts analysis will also examine whether or not the claim "arises out of" the defendant's contact with the forum state. Here, the claim arises directly out of Smith Dolls' contact with State X. Smith Dolls sold Little Tracy dolls to a toy store in State X. Sarah Simpson choked on a piece of one of the dolls and died as a result. It is difficult to see how a legal claim could be any more closely related to the contacts with the forum.

Small burden on defendant

Also important to a minimum contacts analysis is the burden that the defendant will sustain in defending itself in the plaintiff's choice of forum. Here, it is unlikely that Smith Dolls will be able to demonstrate a significant burden. State Y is only 500 miles from State X. Furthermore, in this technologically advanced age, it is not difficult for a defendant to defend itself in a jurisdiction other than its home state, unless the forum state is quite distant (which is probably not the case here).

Domicile has interest in redressing plaintiff's harm

Finally, State X probably will want to hear the case. As the plaintiff's domicile, the state will have an interest in addressing the plaintiff's concerns.

Foreseeability

Under a foreseeability analysis, it is also likely that State X will have jurisdiction over the case. The facts state that there have been a number of choking incidents with Little Tracy dolls, since Smith Dolls presumably has notice of the dolls' dangerous features, then, and as Smith Dolls knows that its dolls are being sold in State X (by virtue of the fact that the company shipped dolls on five occasions in the past year to a State X toy store), Smith Dolls should be able to foresee that an injury would occur in State X and that a lawsuit might be brought there.

A good student would note, however, that, unless the Simpsons had serious transportation problems, they probably would have wanted to bring their case in State Y to ensure that the law of State Y was applied. The law of State Y allows them to recover far more in damages than does the law in State X. This was probably a strategic error on the part of their attorney.

2. Assume for the purposes of this question only that the State X court does have jurisdiction over the case and uses a vested rights approach to choice of law in this case. What law will apply? What are the pros and cons of this approach?

Characterization

Under a vested rights approach, in order to decide what law to apply, the court will first characterize the case. The State X court is likely to characterize this case as a tort case, because the claim is for wrongful death and because Sarah was injured by choking on a doll shoe.

Choice of law

If the case is indeed characterized as a tort case, the court will then look to see what most proximate act created liability. Under this analysis the court usually looks to the law of the state where the injury occurred. Because Sarah's death occurred in State X, the court will probably choose to apply the law of State X.

Escape device

The Simpsons' lawyer will probably move the court to apply the law of State Y, as that law is far more favorable to the Simpsons, allowing them to recover up to $5,000,000 rather than only $100,000. However, under a vested rights approach, in order to apply State Y's law, the court will need to recharacterize the case as some other type of case. For example, were the court to characterize the case as a contract case, it might be able to argue that State Y's law should apply (although even this would be a stretch, given that the case would probably be considered to involve a breach issue, and breach issues are usually controlled by the law of the state where the breach occurred).

When a court characterizes a case in a non-intuitive way in order to achieve a certain result, it is said to employ an "escape device."

Pros of the vested rights approach

There are few pros to the vested rights approach for the Simpsons, as the results of the choice of law are not as favorable to them under this approach. However, one pro would certainly be that their lawyer would be quite familiar with the laws of State X, probably far more so than a State Y lawyer who would be defending Smith Dolls. In general, a pro of the vested rights approach is that it provides certain guidelines about which law to apply.

Cons of the vested rights approach

This approach would probably be less than advantageous for the Simpsons because they would really want the law of State Y to apply to increase their potential recovery.

Furthermore, vested rights is a very rigid approach. Therefore, the Simpsons' attorney will probably want to move the court to use a different choice of law approach.

In general, the vested rights approach has several cons. Because it is so rigid, it often leads to the application of law that is not particularly relevant or fair. Furthermore, because judges know that it may yield an undesirable result, it is more likely to be manipulated through the use of escape devices.

3. **Assume for the purposes of this question only that the State X court does have jurisdiction over the case and uses a most significant relationship approach to choice of law in this case. What law will apply? What are the pros and cons of this approach?**

Choice of law

Under the most significant relationship approach, the State X court will apply the law of the state that it views to be most integrally connected to the Simpsons' dispute with Smith Dolls. In other words, the court will look at which state's contacts are more significant than the other's. Under this very flexible approach, it is likely that the court could go either way in deciding which law to apply. On the one hand, Sarah lived her whole life in State X, her parents live there, the Little Tracy doll was purchased there, and the injury occurred there. On the other hand, Smith Dolls is located and incorporated in State Y, the Little Tracy doll that led to Sarah's death was made there, and the doll was shipped from there.

It should be obvious from this analysis that, under the most significant relationship approach, the State X court will have ample freedom in deciding which law to apply.

Pros of the most significant relationship approach

The most significant relationship approach will probably be better for the Simpsons than the vested rights approach because it is much more flexible, and the court will have more leeway in deciding which law to apply. The court could conceivably give more weight to the contacts with State Y and apply that state's more favorable law.

Cons of the most significant relationship approach

Working against the Simpsons is the fact that, on the face of it, it appears that their claim has more contacts in State X than in State Y. Furthermore, a con of the approach is that under this approach the laws are easier to manipulate to achieve a desired result.

4. **Assume for the purposes of this question only that the State X court does have jurisdiction over the case and uses a better law approach to choice of law in this case. What law will apply? What are the pros and cons of this approach?**

Choice of law

If it employs a better law approach, the State X court's choice of law will depend on which law the court views as "better." The better law approach takes into account the fact that judges can manipulate the outcome of a case through the choice of applicable law; therefore, under the better law approach, the court looks at the end result of each choice of law and chooses the law that yields the better outcome.

In this case, then, under a better law approach, the State X court will essentially look at the outcome of the case under both State X law and State Y law. It might also look at which state's law is the majority rule or a particularly intriguing and persuasive minority rule. It can also look at the fairness of the result the application of the law would yield.

In many cases, a court using a better law approach will choose the law of the forum state, perhaps because that law has been developed with policy reasons in mind. However, this is not always the case. In the Simpson case, if the court feels that plaintiffs in wrongful death suits should receive large damage awards, it may choose to apply the law of State Y.

Pros of the better law approach

For the Simpsons, the benefit of the better law approach is that the judge may explicitly look at the outcome when choosing the law. Therefore, a "plaintiff's" judge may choose the law of State Y, particularly if the statute there is similar to statutes in many other jurisdictions. In general, better law proponents say that judges can be honest about their biases under this approach.

Cons of the better law approach

Simplification of the judicial task to does not necessarily guarantee more predictable results or arrival at the most "reasonable and sensible law."

5. Does the Pistonacre state court have jurisdiction over the case?

It is questionable whether the Pistonacre state court would have jurisdiction over the case.

Minimum contacts

About the only contact that the used car dealer had with Pistonacre was the online auction. Other than that, so far as we know, the dealer has not done much business in Pistonacre. Furthermore, the dealer did not visit Pistonacre at any point. Therefore, it is unclear whether the court will consider a single sale to a Pistonacre resident to constitute adequate contact with the forum. Under Supreme Court precedent, it seems unlikely.

Claim arises out of contacts

A minimum contacts analysis will also examine whether or not the claim "arises out of" the defendant's contact with the forum state. Here, the claim arose out of the explosion that occurred in Pistonacre. The explosion was the result of the sale of the car to a Pistonacre resident. However, as the sale occurred in Gasacre, it is still questionable whether the claim arises out of the contact.

Small burden on defendant

Also important to a minimum contacts analysis is the burden that the defendant will sustain in defending itself in the plaintiff's choice of forum. This factor will play in the plaintiff's favor. As a "neighboring state," Gasacre is right next door to Pistonacre. To travel to Pistonacre to defend itself probably will not be a significant burden for the dealer.

Domicile has interest in redressing plaintiff's harm

Finally, Pistonacre probably will want to hear the case. As the plaintiff's domicile, that state will have an interest in addressing the plaintiff's concerns.

Foreseeability

Under a foreseeability analysis, it is questionable whether Pistonacre will have jurisdiction over the case. The facts state that there was an explosion, but they do not state whether or not the used car dealer knew that an explosion was likely to happen due to a known defect or other problem. If the dealership did know (or should have known) about the potential for explosion, then the suit in Pistonacre is likely to be seen as foreseeable. If, however, the explosion was due to a hidden defect or a fluke, then the lawsuit is likely not to have been foreseeable.

Conclusion

For all of these reasons, it is unclear whether Pistonacre will be able to assert jurisdiction over the case. If the used car dealer were to move to dismiss on jurisdictional grounds, he would likely prevail.

6. **Assume for the purposes of this question only that the Pistonacre court does have jurisdiction over the case and uses a "lex fori" approach to choice of law in this case. What law will apply? What are the pros and cons of this approach?**

Application of the "lex fori" approach

Were the Pistonacre court to use a "lex fori" choice of law approach in this case, Myers will probably be extremely pleased. If the court uses this approach, it would be among a very small minority of states that virtually always apply the law of the forum. In other words, in "lex fori" jurisdictions, there actually is no choice of law in substantive law situations. A "lex fori" jurisdiction is quite up front about the fact that it will always apply its own substantive law, as long as to do so is constitutional.

Of course, even in a "lex fori" jurisdiction, where a court presumes that it will apply its own substantive law, the opposing party may contest that choice of law and persuade the court to use another choice of law approach. For this reason, "lex fori" is a presumption, but it is a rebuttable presumption. For example, in a situation where a forum had no contacts whatsoever with the claim, the opposing party might be able to rebut the court's presumption that it would apply forum law.

Pros of the "lex fori" approach

For Jonathan Myers, the "lex fori" approach would be extremely advantageous. Pistonacre allows lemon law claims, even where the contract does not explicitly provide for them. On the other hand, Gasacre does not allow such claims. Myers will obviously want Pistonacre law to apply. Therefore, his attorney has probably made an excellent decision in bringing Myers' claim in Pistonacre.

Cons of the "lex fori" approach

Although there is little downside for Myers in application of the "lex fori" approach, there are cons in general. The approach encourages plaintiffs to forum shop and may result in the application of the law of a forum that has almost no contact with the claim.

7. Is there a true conflict in this case? Why or why not?

Yes, in this case there is probably a true conflict, as both Pistonacre and Gasacre would have an interest in having their law apply. Under interest analysis theory, a true conflict is one in which more than one state has an interest in the court choosing its laws.

Gasacre's interest

Gasacre is probably interested in having its law apply because it wants to protect the used car dealer that is located and incorporated there. Furthermore, its legislators have decided that used car dealers should not bear the burden of liability for injuries that occur after a sale is complete. Requiring Pistonacre's implied warranty policy to apply to Gasacre dealers would be a serious hardship for those dealers, especially given that Gasacre is a neighboring state and could presumably sell many cars to Pistonacre residents.

Pistonacre's interest

Pistonacre is definitely interested in having its law apply. First, Myers, a resident of Pistonacre, suffered damages as a result of the explosion. Second, the explosion occurred in Pistonacre. Third, Pistonacre policy has protected the buyers of used cars. To apply Gasacre law in this situation would leave buyers at risk by potentially having no recourse when they bought unsafe cars.

Resolution

In a true conflict situation like this one, both states have a demonstrated interest in having their law apply. Therefore, absent a vested rights analysis, it may be difficult for a court to decide which law should apply. In these cases, courts often apply the law of the forum, because to do so at least succeeds in advancing the forum's interests and agenda. Therefore, it seems likely that Pistonacre will apply its own law to the dispute, granting Myers a much greater chance of recovery.

8. **Assume for the purposes of this question only that the Pistonacre court does have jurisdiction over the case and uses "depeçage" in this case. What law will apply? What are the pros and cons of this approach?**

"Depeçage"

When a court uses "depeçage" it applies different law to different substantive issues in the case. For example, in this case, under a "depeçage" approach, a court might apply Pistonacre's law to a breach of implied warranty claim and Gasacre's law to a straight breach of contract or tort claim. Such application of different law to different issues is sometimes called "issue splitting."

Pros of "depeçage"

"Depeçage" can be a very advantageous approach because it essentially allows the court to decide what is the better law for each issue in the lawsuit or allows the parties to demonstrate that, with respect to different issues, different states may have the "most significant relationship." In this way, "depeçage" differs from vested rights, in which a single forum's law must apply to the entire controversy. Many "depeçage" proponents advance the view that the use of this approach allows the court to reach fairer, more balanced decisions. The Second Restatement solidly backs this approach.

Cons of "depeçage"

On the other hand, some courts feel that application of "depeçage" means that state policy will be diluted in all cases and that no state will fully achieve its policy goals. Such dissenters feel that a court must make a choice about which state's law should apply exclusively to the entire controversy.

9. What law should the federal district court apply in deciding the motion to dismiss?

Under *Erie* doctrine, the court should apply the Federal Rules of Civil Procedure. The contents of a complaint are a purely procedural requirement. Under *Erie*, where the Federal Rules of Civil Procedure conflict with state procedural rules, the FRCP should apply.

Therefore, because the Federal Rules will apply, the complaint will be adequate, and the motion to dismiss should be denied.

10. Assume for the purposes of this question only that the motion to dismiss is denied. What law should the federal district court apply in deciding the breach of contract claim?

Whether or not the contract was breached will be a question of substantive law. Under *Erie*, because there is little to no federal common law, a federal district court sitting in diversity will generally apply the substantive law of the state in which it sits. For this reason, the court will probably apply the Watercolor Commercial Code.

Cain's lawyer has made a good choice of forum in this case. In fact, *Erie* doctrine may often lead to forum shopping, because, knowing that the federal district court will usually apply the state law of the forum in which it sits, plaintiffs try to bring suits in a forum with favorable substantive law. Here, the Watercolor Commercial Code allows a buyer 150 days to report a defect to the seller. This statute of limitations means that Cain will be able to bring a suit, since he reported the defect approximately 125 days after receiving the painting. On the other hand, had Cain brought his suit in Pastel, the federal district court in Pastel probably would have applied Pastel law, and Cain's claim would have been barred.

Sneak Peak from

Kaplan PMBR FINALS: Constitutional Law

OUTLINE

VI. EQUAL PROTECTION OF THE LAWS

A. CONSTITUTIONAL BASIS

1. **Source:** The 14th Amendment provides that "no state shall ... deny to any person within its jurisdiction the equal protection of the laws."

2. **Relationship between Substantive Due Process and Equal Protection:** The guarantee of substantive due process assures that a law will be fair and reasonable, not arbitrary. Equal protection review is triggered where persons similarly situated are treated differently.

   a. **Substantive due process:** Substantive due process review applies where a law affects the rights of *all* persons with respect to a specific activity (e.g., state law prohibits the sale of birth control devices, except by prescription).

   b. **Equal protection:** Equal protection review applies where a law affects the rights of *some* persons with respect to a specific activity (e.g., state law prohibits the sale of birth control devices to unmarried persons, except by prescription).

B. THREE STANDARDS OF REVIEW

1. **Strict Scrutiny:** *Under the strict scrutiny standard, the burden of persuasion is on the government to prove that the measure being challenged is necessary to further a compelling interest*. The word "necessary" means that there is no less restrictive alternative means available. There must be a very close "fit" between the means and the end. The government usually fails to prove its burden under strict scrutiny, so the Equal Protection challenge to the law is generally a winning argument (i.e., the law is presumptively invalid). *Strict scrutiny review applies to 1) suspect classes — race, alienage, and national origin; 2) fundamental rights — right to vote, right to travel, right to privacy; and 3) protected 1st Amendment rights.*

2. **Middle-tier, or Intermediate, Scrutiny:** *Under the middle-tier standard, the burden of persuasion is generally placed on the government to prove that the measure being challenged is substantially related to an important interest.* The key term, "substantially related", means that an exceedingly persuasive justification must be shown. Middle-tier scrutiny is much closer to strict scrutiny than it is to rational basis. *Intermediate scrutiny applies to classifications based on the following quasi-suspect areas: 1) gender and 2) illegitimacy*; also, a similar, though not identical, test is used for 3) content neutral time, place, manner regulation of free speech.

3. **Rational Basis Scrutiny:** *Under the rational basis standard of review, the burden of persuasion is on the plaintiff to show the measure being challenged is not rationally related to any legitimate interest.* Rational relationship is a minimal requirement which means that the law cannot be arbitrary or unreasonable. Practically any police power regulation which furthers a health, safety, or welfare purpose will be found "legitimate". For this reason, laws scrutinized under rational basis are almost always upheld. From the plaintiff's standpoint rational basis is traditionally a default test (i.e., an equal protection challenge under rational basis is generally a losing argument). *Rational basis review applies to all classifications not falling under strict or intermediate scrutiny, namely such classifications as those based on age, poverty, wealth, mental retardation, necessities of life (food, shelter, clothing, medical care), and social and economic welfare measures.*

C. PROVING DISCRIMINATORY CLASSIFICATIONS

1. **Intentional Discrimination Required:** Discriminatory intent (i.e., purposeful, invidious discrimination) must be shown to trigger strict or intermediate scrutiny. Mere discriminatory effect is insufficient. Discriminatory intent may be shown facially, or as applied, or where a discriminatory motive exists.

   a. **Facial discrimination:** Facial discrimination arises where a law, by its very language, creates distinctions between classes of persons (e.g., only white, male U.S. citizens may apply for positions with the state police department).

   b. **Discriminatory application:** A facially neutral law can be applied in a discriminatory manner. Where the challenger can show a discriminatory purpose, the law will be invalidated. [*Yick Ho v. Hopkins*, 118 U.S. 356 (1886) — law prohibiting operation of laundries in wooden buildings most of which were owned by Chinese individuals, but granting discretionary exemptions, held invalid].

   c. **Discriminatory motive:** Where a law which appears neutral on its face and in its application has a disproportionate effect on a particular class of persons, strict or middle-tier scrutiny will apply only if the Court finds a *discriminatory purpose* exists. [*Washington v. Davis*, 426 U.S. 229 (1976) — the fact that black applicants on a police qualifying test scored lower than white applicants did not per se prove a discriminatory purpose in hiring practices, so strict scrutiny review was not triggered and no Equal Protection violation was found].

D. SUSPECT CLASSIFICATIONS

1. **Race and National Origin:** Strict scrutiny applies to classifications based on race and national origin. Such laws will be presumptively invalid, absent a showing by the state that the measure is necessary to a compelling interest.

a. **Racial (or ethnic) classifications:** A state law prohibiting interracial marriages was held unconstitutional [*Loving v. Virginia*, 388 U.S. 1 (1967)]; and a state law prohibiting interracial cohabitation was held invalid. [*McLaughlin v. Florida*, 379 U.S. 184 (1964)].

b. **School segregation:** In *Brown v. Board of Education*, 347 U.S. 483 (1954), which overruled *Plessy v. Ferguson*, 163 U.S. 537 (1896), the Court held that deliberate "de jure" segregation violates equal protection. Also, various plans to hinder desegregation have been deemed unconstitutional, including the closing of all public schools. [*Griffin v. County School Board of Prince Edward County*, 377 U.S. 218 (1964)] and in [*Norwood v. Harrison*, 413 U.S. 455 (1973)], the Court held public aid to private segregated schools (such as tuition grants and exclusive use of public facilities) unconstitutional.

  (1) **Busing:** School boards have an affirmative duty to eliminate intentional racial segregation of schools. Court-ordered busing is constitutional where it is implemented to remedy past discrimination in a particular school system. Court-ordered busing is a temporary measure which must be terminated once the vestiges of past discrimination have been eliminated. [*Board of Education v. Dowell*, 498 U.S. 237 (1991)]. Also, the proper purpose of court-ordered busing must be to remedy past discrimination, not to attract non-minority students from outside districts to achieve integration.

c. **Affirmative Action:** In *Richmond v. Croson*, 488 U.S. 469 (1989), the USSC first held that minority set-asides established by state or local governments for construction projects—i.e., programs where a fixed percentage of publicly funded money is awarded to minority-owned businesses—are subject to strict scrutiny review and must be narrowly tailored to justify a compelling interest. Subsequently, in *Adarand Construction, Inc v. Pena*, 515 U.S. 200 (1995) the Court set forth a clear rule that ***any race-based affirmative action program designed to remedy past discrimination—whether enacted by a state municipality, or even the federal government—is subject to strict scrutiny.*** This rule applies to any "benign", or compensatory, program by any government entity which either ***favors or discriminates against*** racial or ethnic minorities. Other general principles include the following:

  (1) Remedying past discrimination in a particular government institution is generally viewed as a compelling interest, but attempting to remedy general, societal injustice through affirmative action is not.

  (2) Race or ethnic origin may be considered as a factor in admissions programs — *U.C. Regents v. Bakke*, 438 U.S. 265 (1978) — ***but use of "quota" systems (as opposed to hiring "goals") is disfavored and will almost always be struck down as not being necessary to promote racial***

equality or educational diversity. Bakke was affirmed in *Grutter v. Bollinger*, 123 S. Ct. 2325 (2003) (school may take race into account as one of many factors in making admissions decisions); but *see Gratz v. Bollinger*, 123 S. Ct. 2411 (2003) (school may not use quota system to enroll minority students, even if expressed purpose is to remedy past discrimination and create a diverse student body).

(3) Discrimination by private employers is not subject to equal protection review, but may be restricted under the 13th Amendment or the Commerce Clause.

d. **Racial gerrymandering:** Where it can be shown that race was the "predominant factor" in defining the borders of new election districts (rather than contiguity, compactness, or community interest), then such a plan will violate strict scrutiny absent a showing by the state that the scheme was narrowly tailored to serve a compelling interest. [*Miller v. Johnson*, 515 U.S. 900 (1995)].

2. **Alienage:** Although alienage is not a "suspect" classification per se, the Court will generally apply the strict scrutiny test where a state law discriminates against aliens.

Examples: A state law prohibiting aliens from owning land was invalidated in *Oyama v. California*, 332 U.S. 633 (1948); and a state law denying commercial fishing licenses to resident aliens, who were ineligible for citizenship, held invalid [*Takahashi v. Fish & Game Commission*, 334 U.S. 410 (1948)]; and in *Nyquist v. Mauclet*, 432 U.S. 1 (1977), the Court invalidated a state law that excluded financial assistance for higher education to aliens who were eligible for U.S. citizenship as not furthering any "compelling state interest."

Exception: States may discriminate against aliens where participation in the functioning of government is involved: New York statute requiring state police officers to be citizens held valid. [*Foley v. Connelie*, 435 U.S. 291 (1978)]; also, aliens may be denied positions as public school teachers because they may influence students' views toward government and the political process. [*Ambach v. Norwick*, 441 U.S. 68 (1979)].

Illegal Aliens: The USSC has not held illegal aliens to be a suspect class. Rational basis analysis applies. However, note that in *Plyler v. Doe*, 457 U.S. 202 (1982), the Court determined that illegal alien children have a right to free public elementary and secondary education.

Note: Remember that federal classifications based upon alienage are not subject to the strict scrutiny test, because Congress has broad plenary power to regulate immigration. Thus, in *Mathews v. Diaz*, 426 U.S. 67 (1976), Congress established a five-year residency requirement for federal Medicare benefits that disqualified many resident aliens. On the other hand, in *Hampton v. Moo Sun Wong*, 426 U.S.

88 (1976), the Court barred discrimination against aliens in federal civil service employment.

3. **Illegitimacy:** Distinctions drawn between legitimate and illegitimate children are subject to an intermediate, or "quasi-suspect," standard. [*Mathews v. Lucas,* 427 U.S. 495 (1976)]. As a result, it is now close to the "almost suspect" standard used for gender discrimination. [*Mills v. Habluetzel,* 102 S. Ct. 1549 (1982) — classifications must be "substantially related to an important state interest"]. Classifications that favor legitimates and disfavor illegitimates are generally struck down since the overriding government interest in this area is not to punish the offspring of an illicit relationship.

   a. **Wrongful death:** In *Levy v. Louisiana,* 391 U.S. 68 (1968), the Court struck down a state law which permitted legitimate children (but not illegitimate children) to maintain a wrongful death action.

   b. **Workmen's compensation:** Similarly, in *Weber v. Aetna Casualty and Surety Company,* 406 U.S. 164 (1972), the Court invalidated a state law that excluded illegitimate children from sharing equally with other children in worker's compensation death benefits.

   c. **Welfare benefits:** Likewise, illegitimate children are entitled to welfare benefits. [*New Jersey Welfare Rights Organization v. Cahill,* 411 U.S. 619 (1973)].

   d. **Intestate succession:** Illinois intestacy statute, which excluded illegitimate children from inheriting from their intestate fathers, was declared unconstitutional. [*Trimble v. Gordon,* 430 U.S. 762 (1977)]: however, in *Lalli v. Lalli,* 439 U.S. 259 (1978), the Court upheld a New York intestacy statute that required the paternity of the father be proved during his lifetime, as serving an important state interest in promoting a just or orderly disposition of property at death.

   Note: As with federal classifications based upon alienage, the Supreme Court has been more lenient in applying an intermediate standard of scrutiny to illegitimacy under federal law than under state law. The Court upheld a federal law granting immigration preferences to legitimate children in *Fiallo v. Bell,* 430 U.S. 787 (1977) — within Congress's plenary power to regulate immigration.

4. **Gender:** Classifications based on gender are *"quasi-suspect" and violate equal protection unless they are "substantially related to important government interests."* [*Craig v. Boren,* 429 U.S. 190 (1976) — Oklahoma statute, which permitted the sale of beer to females over 18 years old but forbade the sale of the beverage to males between 18 and 21, held invalid as *not* substantially related to any important government objectives]. Middle-tier review applies whether

the classification is invidious (intended to harm) or benign (intended to help, or intended to remedy past discrimination). Intentional, or purposeful, discrimination is required to trigger middle-tier scrutiny; just as was discussed regarding race, discriminatory effect alone is insufficient. Statutes which reinforce archaic gender-based stereotypes will almost certainly be struck down. Based on an important recent decision, the Court will apply intermediate scrutiny in a quite rigorous manner such that the ***government*** must prove gender discrimination and show that an "exceedingly persuasive justification" exists. [*U.S. v. Virginia*, 518 U.S. 515 (1996)].

a. **Discrimination against women:** In recent decisions, the Court has held unconstitutional under equal protection all laws discriminating against women. A state law giving preference to men over women (who were equally qualified) to be administrators of decedents' estates held unconstitutional in *Reed v. Reed,* 404 U.S. 71 (1971)]; also in *Frontiero v. Richardson,* 411 U.S. 677 (1973) discrimination in military benefits to servicewomen held invalid.

b. **Discrimination against men:** The Court has held unconstitutional under equal protection laws discriminating against men. [*Craig v. Boren, supra];* also, the Court struck down a law authorizing alimony payments upon divorce to women but not to men. [*Orr v. Orr,* 440 U.S. 268 (1979)]; and in *Caban v. Mohammed,* 441 U.S. 380 (1979) — the Court invalidated a New York law that permitted an unwed mother, but not an unwed father, to block the adoption of their child]; and recently in *Mississippi University for Women v. Hogan,* 102 S. Ct. 3331 (1982), the Court held the exclusion of males from a state nursing school violated a male applicant's right to equal protection.

Caveat: Note, however, that in some cases laws discriminating against men have been upheld when "substantially related to important government objectives." In *Rostker v. Goldberg,* 453 U.S. 57 (1981), for example, the Court upheld the registration of males and not females for conscription by the military because Congress, pursuant to its military powers, has determined that this was necessary to further important government interests; also, in *Michael M. v. Sonoma County Superior Court,* 450 U.S. 464 (1981), statutory rape laws that punished the male participant (but not the female accessory) upheld because it furthered an important state interest in preventing teenage pregnancy.

c. **Benign sex discrimination:** Such laws are generally upheld as being substantially related to the important governmental objective of ameliorating past gender-based discrimination. Thus, in *Califano v. Webster,* 430 U.S. 313 (1977), Social Security statutes and tax exemptions that entitle women to greater benefits were upheld; also, a navy discharge procedure that required male officers, who were twice denied promotion, to be automatically discharged (whereas female officers were not) was upheld in *Schlesinger v. Ballard,* 419 U.S. 498 (1975), because in the past men were afforded greater promotional opportunities than women.

5. **Age:** Age is not a "suspect" classification. The Court has upheld the validity of a Massachusetts statute requiring police officers to retire at age 50, even though they may be as physically fit as younger officers. [*Massachusetts Board of Retirement v. Murgia,* 427 U.S. 307 (1976)]. Thus, laws and other governmental action against the elderly are judged by the traditional (or "rational basis") test.

6. **Poverty:** The Court has held that "poverty standing alone is not a suspect classification." [*Harris v. McRae,* 448 U.S. 297 (1980)]; and in *James v. Valtierra,* 402 U.S. 137 (1971), the Court upheld a state law that required approval by a local referendum as a prerequisite for the construction of low-rent public housing projects.

7. **Mental retardation:** In *City of Cleburne v. Cleburne Living Center,* 473 U.S. 432, (1985), the Court held that mental retardation is not a "quasi-suspect" classification, and that the rational basis standard of review is applicable.

Questions 1–2 are based on the following fact situation.

North Berlin, an industrial town with a population of 100,000, is located on the north side of the Germantown River. On the south side of the river is situated South Berlin, a rural community with a population of 40,000. For many years, various civic groups have urged that both communities merge into one township with a single governmental body. Independent studies have indicated that such a merger would result in an enormous tax savings to the residents of both municipalities by eliminating the duplication of services. On one previous occasion, proponents of the merger plan succeeded in having the proposal appear as an election referendum in each community. Although the merger referendum passed in North Berlin by a sizable margin, the voters of South Berlin rejected the measure, fearing the combined government would be dominated and controlled by its neighbor's larger representation.

In order to alleviate the concern of South Berlin voters regarding underrepresentation in a merged governmental system, the respective city councils of both municipalities appointed a steering committee to formulate a new proposal. Accordingly, the steering committee devised a merger scheme wherein the city council of Berlin, the united city, would consist of eight members. Within this proposed new system of government, each former municipality would be divided into four districts. With respect to North Berlin, each district would consist of 25,000 persons and each would have one elected city council member. By the same token, South Berlin would be divided into four elective districts with each containing 10,000 residents. One city council member would be elected from each of these districts as well. The mayor would be elected at large by a popular vote of all residents in the newly created eight districts.

Before this merger proposal was placed on the ballot, the state attorney general issued an advisory opinion stating that the measure did not, in her opinion, violate any statutory or constitutional provisions. Thereafter, the "Berlin Proposal," as it came to be known, was placed on the ballot and was overwhelmingly passed by the voters in both North Berlin and South Berlin. After the election but before the merger had officially been carried out, two taxpayers from North Berlin initiated suit to enjoin the unification, attacking the constitutionality of the disproportionate representative districts.

1. Which of the following represents the plaintiffs' strongest constitutional argument in support of their action?

   (A) The plaintiffs and other North Berlin residents have been denied the equal protection of the law.
   (B) The plaintiffs and other North Berlin residents have been denied the due process of the law.
   (C) The plaintiffs and other North Berlin residents have been denied the privileges and immunities of citizenship as guaranteed by Article IV, Section 2.
   (D) The merged city "Berlin Proposal" would not constitute a republican form of government.

2. Assume for the purposes of this question only that the plaintiffs' suit reaches the state supreme court and that the court ruled the "Berlin Proposal" establishing a unified city entity was constitutional under both the state and the federal constitutions. The plaintiffs now file a motion seeking to have this case reviewed by the U.S. Supreme Court. The Court should

(A) hear the federal issues involved, but decline to rule on the state issue
(B) not hear the case, but have it remanded to federal district court
(C) not hear the case, because it was decided on independent state grounds
(D) rely on the advisory opinion rendered by the state attorney general and not hear the case on its merits

Question 3 is based on the following fact situation.

3. Congress has recently enacted a federal law that prohibits racial discrimination in the sale, transfer, or rental of real estate, either privately or publicly. Which of the following constitutional provisions would provide the best rationale for the enactment of this federal statute?

(A) Under Article I Congress has the power to enact laws that are "necessary and proper" to the general welfare.
(B) The enforcement provision of Section 2 of the 13th Amendment.
(C) The enforcement provision of Section 5 of the 14th Amendment.
(D) The due process clause of the 5th Amendment.

Question 4 is based on the following fact situation.

4. In which instance would a state, under the enabling clause of the 14th Amendment, be most able to regulate?

(A) A private individual from discriminating against a Black.
(B) A private individual from discriminating against a Mexican.
(C) A state official from discriminating against an Asian.
(D) A federal official from discriminating against a Black.

1. (A)

State control over the right to vote is not expressly limited by the federal constitution. However, any inequality in allocating the right to vote based on using electoral districts established on criteria other than street population dilutes the "one man, one vote" principle and will be subject to strict scrutiny review by the Court. In *Reynolds v. Sims*, 377 U.S. 533 (1964), Justice Warren formulated the one person, one vote rule: "If a State should provide that the votes of citizens in one part of the State should be given two times, or five times, or 10 times the weight of votes of citizens in another part of the State, it could hardly be contended that the right to vote of those residing in the disfavored areas had not been effectively diluted. The Equal Protection Clause requires that the seats in both houses of a bicameral state legislature must be apportioned on a population basis." Nowak, **Constitutional Law,** p. 754.

2. (A)

If *a state court holds a state law valid under both state and federal constitutional provisions*, then the Supreme Court *may* exercise review. Specifically, if the Court *disagreed* with the state court's review of the *federal constitution,* the state decision would have to be reversed regardless of the interpretation of the state law. Therefore, the doctrine of adequate state grounds would not apply, and the Court would hear the federal issues presented. In this question, if the state court improperly interpreted federal law—namely the Equal Protection issue arising from the diluted reapportionment scheme under the "Berlin Proposal"—then the Supreme Court would hear the case and reverse the state court's decision. Choice (A) is thus correct.

3. (B)

The 13th Amendment is unique in two respects. First, it contains an absolute bar to the existence of slavery or involuntary servitude; there is no requirement of "state action." *Thus, it is applicable to individuals as well as states.* Secondly, like the 14th and 15th Amendments, it contains an enforcement clause, enabling Congress to pass all necessary legislation. In this regard, the Court has held that the enforcement provision of the 13th Amendment has extended Section 1982 of the 1866 Civil Rights Act "to insure minorities the freedom to inherit, purchase, lease, sell, hold and convey real and personal property." Most importantly, the 13th Amendment has been construed to prohibit both public and private racial discrimination in housing.

4. (C)

The most clear case where a state can regulate to protect one's constitutional rights under the 14th Amendment occurs when state action is involved. Thus, choices (A) and (B) are incorrect because private discrimination is involved. Choice (D) is likewise wrong because a federal official is doing the discriminating. Consequently, choice (C) is the *best* answer because a state is most able to regulate the actions of a state official when these actions violate one's constitutional rights.

Sneak Peak from

Kaplan PMBR FINALS: Property

VII. MORTGAGES

A. IN GENERAL

1. Definition

A *mortgage* is an interest in land created by a written instrument providing security for the performance of a duty or the payment of a debt. If the *mortgagor* does not pay the mortgage debt on time, the *mortgagee* (or the party to whom the debt is owned) has two choices. It can either assume title to the piece of real property or call the property to be sold and keep the proceeds toward satisfaction of the mortgage debt.

2. Parties Involved in Transaction

The *mortgagor* creates the mortgage. He is the "landowner" and debtor. The *mortgagee* is the creditor (e.g., bank) and the holder of the mortgage.

3. Types of Mortgage Theories

a. Lien Theory Jurisdiction

In the majority of states, the mortgage creates only a lien on the land regardless of the operative words of the mortgage instrument. Under lien theory, the mortgagor remains the owner of the land, and the mortgagee holds only a security interest in the land. Therefore, the mortgagor retains possession unless a foreclosure takes place, in which case the mortgagee may take over possession of the land.

b. Title Theory Jurisdiction

At common law, and still in about 20 states, the mortgage operates as a ***conveyance of the legal title to the mortgagee***. Note, however, that such title is subject to defeasance on payment of the mortgage debt. However, under a title theory, the mortgagee is actually entitled to possession of the land at any time. Practically, this means that the mortgagee may take possession immediately upon default and need not wait for foreclosure.

c. Distinction Between Lien Theory and Title Theory

For practical purposes, the difference between lien theory and title theory states is not great. Insofar as the substantive rights of the parties are concerned, even in title theory states it is universally recognized that the mortgagee's title is only for purposes of security.

d. **Intermediate Theory Jurisdiction:** Very few states follow the intermediate theory, which states that, while title is in the mortgagor until default, upon default, legal title switches to the mortgagee. Therefore, as in title theory jurisdictions, the mortgagee may take over possession of the property immediately upon default. Note that the difference between intermediate theory and title theory is mostly semantic.

4. **Conveyance of Encumbered Property**

Where a mortgage exists on property at the time that the mortgagor conveys the property to a third party, the language in the deed controls whether the third party assumes liability for the mortgage debt. At common law, the mortgagee could not object to the mortgagor's transfer of the property.

a. **"Subject to" Mortgage**

In a conveyance of land where the deed states that the buyer or grantee takes "subject to" a mortgage, the grantee is *not personally* liable (i.e., *in personam*) for the mortgage debt. However, if she does not pay the debt, the mortgage may be foreclosed and she (the grantee) will lose the land.

b. **"Assumption" of Mortgage**

In a sale of land in which the deed states that the purchaser "assumes" the mortgage, the purchaser or grantee *is personally* liable for the mortgage debt and is subject to a deficiency judgment in the event that a foreclosure sale does not satisfy the debt.

Note: Where the grantee assumes the mortgage but does not pay, she is primarily liable to the mortgagee, but the original mortgagor remains secondarily liable and may be called to pay if the mortgagee does not exceed as against the grantee. Note also that the mortgagee and grantee can contract so that the original mortgagor retains no liability.

c. **Deed Language Is Silent**

Where the deed language is silent, the grantee is considered to take "subject to" the mortgage.

d. **Due-On-Sale Clauses: Modern Law**

Modernly, "subject to" and "assume" do not have much relevance in deeds because a mortgagee will call in the loan and require its full payment when the mortgagor wishes to transfer ownership of the property without the mortgagee's consent. Such clauses have been deemed to be enforceable and operate almost universally in all states today.

e. **Assignments**

Mortgages are assignable. Both the mortgage (i.e., the security) and the note (i.e., the debt) are transferable.

Caveat: When there is a purported transfer of the note or debt to one party, and an assignment of the mortgage to another, the general rule is that the mortgage follows the note or debt. Be aware that the debt or note is the principal relationship, and the mortgage is only ancillary thereto for purposes of security.

f. **Recording**

The mortgage (as well as any assignments thereof) should be recorded. Failure to record the mortgage may make it possible for the mortgagor to convey to a bona fide purchaser ("BFP") who would take free of the mortgage under the recording act.

5. **Equity of Redemption**

The term *equity of redemption* refers to the interest of the mortgagor in a title jurisdiction after default. It was in this situation that the mortgagor needed the aid of equity to provide relief from the conveyance, which at law had become absolute in the mortgagee.

a. **Meaning of Term "Equity"**

In this situation, the term "equity" is commonly used to refer to the value of the mortgagor's interest over and above the amount of the debt owing to the mortgagee. For example, when the mortgagee under a deed transfers to a BFP, the mortgagor has no rights against the BFP, but he does have an action for redemption against the mortgagee for the value of the land or, at his election, the proceeds of the sale.

Rationale: The mortgagee now has the value of the land in his hands as a separate fund, and the mortgagor may redeem such fund as a substitute for the land.

6. **Foreclosure**

a. **Modern-Day Application**

In most jurisdictions today, foreclosure is the method by which the security (i.e., the mortgaged property), or proceeds from the sale thereof, is applied to the satisfaction of the debt or obligation. It is also the means by which the mortgagee succeeds in ending the mortgagor's ownership interest in the real estate. Before a foreclosure may take place, the mortgagor must default on the loan.

b. **Right of Redemption**

The right of redemption allows a mortgagor in default to pay off the amount owed to the mortgagee and any interest prior to foreclosure. If the mortgagor actually pays off the debt prior to the foreclosure, he redeems the mortgage and takes the land free of the mortgage even though he had previously defaulted.

(1) **Equitable redemption:** Under equitable redemption, the mortgagor must redeem before the foreclosure sale. Once the foreclosure sale has occurred, the mortgagor's rights to redeem are terminated.

(2) **Statutory redemption:** Under a statutory redemption theory, a mortgagor may redeem even after the foreclosure sale has occurred. This period is usually six months to a year. About fifty percent of the states grant the mortgagor a right of statutory redemption.

(3) **Clogging:** A mortgage may not contain a provision that the mortgagor waives the right to redeem. This type of clause is called "clogging" and is invalid. If the mortgagor would like to, however, he may waive the right to redeem *after* the mortgage has been executed in exchange for good and valuable consideration.

c. **Common Law or "Strict Foreclosure" View**

In early times, foreclosure meant literally foreclosing or barring the equity of redemption. It was a remedy afforded the mortgagee to prevent the mortgagor from redeeming his land after default. In other words, the mortgagee sought and obtained a decree to the effect that if the mortgagor did not satisfy the mortgage debt by a specified date, then he would be foreclosed (or barred) from ever redeeming, or getting his land back mortgage-free. This is the so-called "strict foreclosure" view and is still applicable in a minority of states.

d. **Other Methods of Foreclosure**

In some states, other methods of foreclosure (such as foreclosure under power of sale and foreclosure by entry) are available. **Note:** Foreclosure by sale under judicial supervision facilitates the determination of the value of the mortgaged property and thus aids in the determination of the amount of any deficiency decree that might be awarded where the proceeds realized from the sale are insufficient to satisfy the mortgage debt.

e. **Priority**

(1) **Typical order of priority:** Typically, chronology determines the order of priority that various mortgagees hold in the property. The first mortgagee to grant a mortgage to the mortgagor has highest priority, followed by the second mortgagee, followed by the third, and so on. However, this order of priority may be modified in several instances: (1) where a senior mortgagee does not record his mortgage interest (see section on recording statutes); (2) where the senior mortgagee contracts away his priority to a junior mortgagee; (3) where a purchase money mortgage is in effect (see below); or (4) where the senior mortgagee changes some condition on the mortgage to make it more difficult for the mortgagor to pay.

(2) **Senior interests:** A prior mortgagee cannot be made a party against his will to a foreclosure action by a "junior mortgagee or encumbrancer." A junior mortgagee or encumbrancer is one who has granted a mortgage to the mortgagor when there was already some outstanding mortgage in place. Thus, the party who extended the original mortgage loan is called a "senior mortgagee" and any subsequent mortgagees are called "junior mortgagees."

(3) **Junior interests:** A junior encumbrancer can be made an involuntary party to a foreclosure action by a senior encumbrancer. In fact, junior encumbrancers must be made parties in order to have their claims eliminated. Where a senior mortgagee does join a junior mortgagee as a party, the junior mortgagee's right to foreclose is completely wiped out.

Note: In a foreclosure sale by a junior encumbrancer or mortgagee, the senior encumbrance or mortgage is unaffected by the proceedings.

(4) **Purchase money mortgages:** Where a mortgagor takes out a loan in order to buy property, this type of mortgage, called a "purchase money mortgage," *takes priority over other types of mortgages, even if those other types of mortgages were recorded earlier in time.*

Note: Purchase money mortgages are heavily tested on the MBE.

7. **Deficiency Judgments**

A deficiency judgment only comes into play when the mortgagor has defaulted in the mortgage debt and the mortgagee has sold the real property at a foreclosure sale. If, at the foreclosure sale, the mortgagee receives enough money for the property to pay off the mortgage debt, the mortgagor has no further obligation. However, where the proceeds from the foreclosure sale do not completely cover the mortgage debt, a deficiency is said to exist. In most states, a mortgagee may proceed directly against the mortgagor for the balance of the loan. This money needed to satisfy the mortgage loan is called a deficiency judgment.

a. **Limitations:** Many states have limitations on the amount a mortgagee may recover for a deficiency judgment. For example, some states limit the amount to the difference between the amount owed and the fair market value of the real estate when the fair market value exceeds the amount brought at the foreclosure sale. Some states even completely forbid deficiency judgment on purchase money mortgages.

8. **Installment Land Sale Contracts**

An installment land sale contract is another kind of security interest. While it is similar to a mortgage, the major difference between an installment land sale contract and a mortgage is that title to the property does not transfer to the buyer until a series of payments has been made. In other words, in a traditional mortgage, a seller sells a piece of property to a buyer, who obtains a mortgage. The buyer makes payments on a monthly basis to a mortgagee. In an installment land sale contract, the buyer makes periodic payments to the seller and does not become the owner of the property until the installments have all been paid. Therefore, the person acquiring the property makes monthly payments just as in a mortgage, but does not have an ownership interest until the debt is fully paid.

Note: Installment land sale contracts have been heavily tested recently on the MBE.

a. **Default:** In an installment land sale contract, where the buyer defaults, several different remedies apply.

(1) **Forfeiture:** Installment land sale contracts usually require that, where a buyer does not make the required payments, she shall forfeit the property. This remedy is the most severe of the various available remedies.

(2) **Grace period:** In many states, a buyer who defaults under an installment land sale contract is granted a grace period to pay off the loan. Such a buyer may keep the land while she is paying under a new payment schedule.

(3) **Forfeiture and restitution:** In some states that require forfeiture of the land, the seller under the installment land sale contract is required to refund to the buyer all installments already paid, as long as these payments are more than the damages suffered by the seller.

(4) **Foreclosure:** In some states, installment land sale contracts are treated as mortgages when the buyer is in default. In these states, the seller must

actually foreclose on the property and sell the property at a foreclosure sale in order to recover money owed.

(5) **Waiver of strict performance:** In many cases of default under an installment land sale contract, a buyer will have made late payments in the past. Where a seller has accepted those late payments, she may be deemed to have waived her right to demand timely payment. In this case, where she wishes the buyer to begin paying in a timely manner, she must send the buyer written notice and allow the buyer a reasonable amount of time to pay back payments owed.

Questions 1–2 are based on the following fact situation.

Quirk owned a four-story office building located in downtown El Paso. The building, named Quirk Towers, was old and badly in need of renovation. To finance the improvements, Quirk borrowed $125,000 from his friend, Lama. As consideration for the loan, Quirk executed a promissory note for $125,000 payable to Lama in one year and secured by a mortgage on Quirk Towers. The mortgage was dated January 1, 1999, and was recorded January 2, 1999. Thereafter, on February 1, 1999, Quirk executed a deed absolute on Quirk Towers and named Lama as grantee. This deed, although absolute in form, was intended only as additional security for the payment of the debt. In order to make judicial foreclosure unnecessary and to eliminate the right to redeem, Quirk then delivered the deed to Uribe in escrow with instructions to deliver the deed to Lama if Quirk failed to pay his promissory note at maturity.

On January 1, 2000, Quirk failed to pay the note when it came due. Thereupon, Uribe, in accordance with escrow instructions, delivered Quirk's deed on the office building to Lama, which he promptly and properly recorded. Two weeks later, Quirk tendered the $125,000 indebtedness to Lama. When Lama refused to accept it, Quirk brought an appropriate action to set aside and cancel the deed absolute and to permit the redemption of Quirk Towers from Lama. Conversely, Lama counterclaimed to quiet title and argued that the deed absolute was intended as an outright conveyance upon default.

1. The court should enter a judgment that will grant the relief sought by

    (A) Quirk, but only if Quirk can establish that the mortgage takes precedence over the deed absolute since it was executed earlier in time
    (B) Quirk, because the deed absolute did not extinguish his right of redemption

    (C) Lama, because the deed absolute effectuated an outright conveyance that extinguished the redemption interest sought to be retained by Quirk
    (D) Lama, because Quirk is estopped to deny the effect of the deed absolute in conjunction with the escrow arrangement

2. For this question only, assume the following facts. On January 1, 2000, Quirk failed to pay the note when it came due. The next day, Uribe, the escrow agent, delivered the deed to Quirk Towers to Lama. Lama then properly recorded this deed on January 3. One week later, on January 10, Lama conveyed Quirk Towers by warranty deed to Gonzales for the purchase price of $200,000. On January 12, Quirk tendered the $125,000 balance due to Lama, which he refused to accept. Quirk now brings an appropriate action against Lama and Gonzales to set aside the conveyance and to permit the redemption of the property by Quirk. Which of the following best states Quirk's legal rights, if any, in his action against Lama and Gonzales?

    (A) Quirk has no rights against Gonzales but Quirk does have an action for redemption against Lama for the value of the property.
    (B) Quirk has no rights against Lama but Quirk does have an action for redemption against Gonzales for the value of the property.
    (C) Quirk has the option of seeking redemption against either Lama or Gonzales for the value of the property but Quirk cannot set aside the conveyance.
    (D) Quirk has no rights against either Lama or Gonzales because he defaulted on the promissory note.

EXPLANATORY ANSWERS

1. (B)

One of the most popular Multistate testing areas deals with mortgages. The reason why mortgage problems are frequently tested on the exam is because the "general" bar review courses provide only a cursory review of this extremely important subject area. In this particular question, it has long been recognized *in equity that a deed absolute intended for security will in fact be construed as a mortgage.* This is not really surprising when it is remembered that the traditional form of the mortgage was a conveyance subject to defeasance, and that the equity of redemption was created by the equity court to protect the mortgagor after default. In order to preserve this equity of redemption various rules were formulated to prevent mortgages from limiting or clogging the equity of redemption. The most common example of such rules is the principle "once a mortgage always a mortgage." This, in effect, means that *a mortgagee cannot circumscribe the mortgagor's right to redeem by disguising the transaction as an outright conveyance.* In this example, the facts indicate that Quirk executed the deed absolute to Lama as additional security. Therefore, the deed will not extinguish Quirk's right of redemption since it (the deed absolute) will be construed as a mortgage and not an outright conveyance.

2. (A)

When the "mortgagee" under a deed absolute mortgage transfers to a bona fide purchaser, the mortgagor has no rights against the bona fide purchaser, but he does have an action for redemption against the "mortgagee" for the value of the land, or, at his election, the proceeds of the sale. The theory is that the mortgagee now has the value of the land in his hands as a separate fund, and such fund as a substitute for the land may be redeemed by the mortgagor. Applying this rule to our given set of facts, Quirk has no right against Gonzales, the bona fide purchaser, but he does have an action for redemption against Lama, the mortgagee.

Sneak Peak from

Kaplan PMBR FINALS: Remedies

I. REQUIREMENTS FOR EQUITABLE REMEDIES

A. JURISDICTIONAL BASIS

1. **In General:** Under the merged system of law and equity, a court of general jurisdiction may render an equitable decree as long as the traditional jurisdictional prerequisites are met.

   a. **Actions *in personam*:** For actions in personam, there must be jurisdiction over the subject matter and jurisdiction over the person (namely, the defendant).

   b. **Actions *in rem*:** For actions in rem (or *quasi in rem*) there must be jurisdiction over the subject matter and the *res* (the thing or property) in dispute.

2. **Equitable Jurisdiction:** Assuming an equity court has such primary jurisdiction, the next question is whether equitable jurisdiction exists. This simply means whether the dispute is one that is traditionally cognizable in equity.

3. **Situations Involving Equitable Jurisdiction:** As a general rule, equitable jurisdiction exists in the following cases:

   a. **No adequate remedy at law:** The traditional view is that before granting equitable relief, the court must find the absence of an adequate legal remedy; *or*

   b. **Actions in which equity developed the substantive law:** There are certain types of action where the remedy has been traditionally equitable in nature (e.g., trusts, divorce, matters relating to fiduciary obligations).

4. **Inadequacy of Legal Remedy:** There is no one formula for determining when a legal remedy is inadequate. However, there are some common patterns where the equitable remedy is usually granted. Courts may seek to determine if the legal remedy is complete, practical, and efficient. Other courts may focus on whether there is a substantial injury for which there is no legal remedy. Here are some illustrations:

   a. The plaintiff is deprived of some thing to which she is entitled, because the defendant has committed a tort or a breach of contract. The legal remedy of damages will not do because she needs the thing itself. Thus, the plaintiff will get equitable relief by way of injunction or specific performance.

   Example: Specific performance of an option contract to purchase stock was granted on a showing that the stock was not traded on the market and was seldom exchanged [*Chadwell v. English*, 652 P.2d 310 (Okla. 1982)].

   Example: Plaintiff, owner of a tomato factory, sues to force defendant-tomato grower to deliver the tomatoes promised in a contract. Although the market value of the promised crop is easily calculable, the unavailability of tomatoes from other sources means that plaintiff necessarily would default on some of its obligations to supply others and would suffer an irreparable loss of reputation thereby. Under these circumstances, specific performance may be appropriate as the legal remedy clearly is inadequate. [*Curlice Bros. v. Catts*, 66 A. 935 (NJ, 1907)].

b. The defendant acts in such a way that the plaintiff may be required to bring more than one suit to effectuate her legal remedy. This is a hardship, and equity may avoid it by awarding more adequate relief.

    Example: If the defendant repeatedly trespasses on the plaintiff's land, equity may enjoin the trespass rather than force repeated actions at law to redress the injury.

c. The plaintiff is entitled either to money or certain performance by the defendant. Money, recoverable at law, would be an entirely adequate remedy, but the defendant is insolvent and it is not collectable. However, the defendant is still capable of rendering the performance to which the plaintiff is entitled as an alternative to the money. Under the circumstances, equity may order performance.

d. The plaintiff is entitled to damages at law, and this would be adequate if damages could be measured with any reasonable degree of accuracy, but, under the facts, damages are so speculative that any award is likely to be inadequate.

5. **Inadequacy Not Enough:** The mere inadequacy or lack of a legal remedy does not, *ipso facto*, establish an absolute right to equitable relief; it only allows the claimant to request it. Relief continues, however, to be largely a matter of judicial discretion. For example, an employer may ask the court to specifically enforce an employment contract, arguing that a legal remedy (i.e., damages) is not adequate because the employee has unique skills. Nonetheless, employment contracts are not specifically enforceable based partly on the difficulty of supervising enforcement of the decree and partly on the undesirability of imposing an employment relationship on persons who are in serious disagreement.

II. INJUNCTIVE RELIEF

A. TYPES OF INJUNCTIONS

1. **Mandatory Injunction.** A mandatory injunction is one that requires the defendant to perform an affirmative act and is enforceable by the contempt power of the court.

    Example: Plaintiff, a 30-year-old male, brings an action against Health Club, an all-women's health facility, to allow him to take aerobics classes there. If the court requires the health club to admit him, it will do so in the form of a mandatory injunction.

Example: Plaintiff, a real estate developer, brings an action against City to allow him to build a new hotel on the City's waterfront. If the court requires City to allow the hotel construction, it will do so in the form of a mandatory injunction.

2. **Prohibitory Injunction.** A prohibitory injunction is one that forbids the defendant from acting.

Example: Plaintiff, a small publishing company, brings an action against defendant, a large publishing company, to keep it from publishing a magazine conceptualized and developed by plaintiff. If the court rules in plaintiff's favor, it will issue a prohibitory injunction.

Example: Plaintiff, a women's health clinic, brings an action against defendant, an antiabortion group, to enjoin it from harassing protesters on the sidewalk in front of the clinic. If the court so enjoins the defendant, it will do so in the form of a prohibitory injunction.

3. **Temporary Restraining Order (TRO) vs. Preliminary Injunction.** Temporary injunctive relief, which can take the form of a temporary restraining order or a preliminary injunction, can perform the valuable task of preserving the status quo while the judicial proceedings are pending.

   a. **Temporary restraining orders.** A TRO may be issued to forestall the occurrence of *imminent irreparable harm* pending a hearing for a preliminary injunction.

      i. **Ex parte orders.** A TRO may be granted *ex parte*, i.e., on affidavits of the complainant without affording the defendant notice or an opportunity to be heard. The plaintiff must, however, make a strong showing as to why such notice and hearing should not be required.

         (a) **Duration.** As a general rule, a TRO is limited to a period of about ten days.

         (b) **Time to take effect.** A TRO does not take effect until the defendant has been notified of its existence.

         (c) **Review by the court.** When a TRO has been issued *ex parte*, upon receiving notice of the order the defendant may request its immediate review.

         (d) **Stays of TROs.** When a defendant requests review of a prohibitory injunction, that injunction is generally not stayed. Mandatory injunctions, however, are generally stayed pending review when so requested by a defendant.

   b. **Preliminary injunctions.** A preliminary injunction (sometimes referred to as a temporary injunction or interlocutory injunction) is distinguishable from

Type of injunction	Characteristics	Duration	Available ex parte?
Mandatory	Requires the defendant to perform an affirmative act.	May be temporary or permanent.	Yes, but difficult to get *ex parte* as it requires an affirmative act on defendant's part.
Prohibitory	Forbids the defendant from continuing to act in a certain way.	May be temporary or permanent.	Yes, but does not take effect until defendant has actual notice of order.
TRO	Issued to forestall the occurrence of an imminent, irreparable harm pending a hearing for a preliminary injunction. Usually prohibitory in nature, but may be mandatory.	Usually no more than ten days, or until defendant is able to be heard, whichever comes first.	Yes, but plaintiff must make a strong showing as to why notice and a hearing should not be required. (i.e., to avoid evasive action by the defendant.)
Preliminary	Usually used to preserve the status quo until a more formal hearing may be held. Usually prohibitory in nature, but may be mandatory.	Until a final hearing on the matter may be held.	No.
Permanent	Permanently requires or forbids some action on the part of the defendant.	Until such time as circumstances change and the parties petition the court for a change in the order.	No.

a TRO in that it is of longer duration and is issued only ***after notice and an adversary hearing***. An ***injunctive bond*** is usually required in the event that the moving party loses the action for permanent injunction and the preliminary injunction causes injury to the enjoined party.

4. **Permanent injunction.** A permanent injunction is intended by the court to be in effect permanently. This does not mean that future circumstances can not cause the court to reverse its decision.

B. INADEQUACY OF LEGAL REMEDY

1. **In General:** A court will enjoin a person from certain conduct or order her to undertake affirmative conduct only when it has been demonstrated that her action or failure to act would cause harm for which there is no adequate legal remedy.

   a. **Grounds for inadequacy:** There are four categories of legal inadequacy that may be sufficient to permit the court to consider issuing injunctive relief:

      i. **Multiplicity of litigation:** Inadequacy may be found if the plaintiff would need to bring multiple or sequential lawsuits in order to take advantage of the legal remedy.

      Example: Equity will enjoin continuing trespasses or blocking of an alley. A good illustration of a continuing trespass occurs when debris is dumped on the plaintiff's land. At least where the plaintiff cannot easily remove the debris herself, courts will issue a mandatory injunction to compel its removal and/or a prohibitory injunction to prohibit further dumping.

      ii. **Difficulty in measuring damages:** When there are significant problems in measuring the damages (i.e., the existence or amount of money damages is speculative or conjectural), the legal remedy may be deemed inadequate.

      iii. **The injury being caused to plaintiff is irreparable:** In many circumstances, damages, though calculable, will not provide an adequate substitute for the loss or harm suffered by the plaintiff.

      Example: Toxic fumes from a factory has the effect of destroying trees, crops, and other vegetation on plaintiff's farm.

      Exam tip: In the case of nuisances, the injunctive remedy in equity is almost always superior to the money remedy at law. The plaintiff in such cases has suffered diminished use and enjoyment of her own land, and, unless it is purely commercial land, it cannot be fully compensated for in money. Thus, in such cases, injunctions are granted willingly where the only issue is adequacy of legal remedy, though they may be denied when factors of hardship or public interest are weighed in the balance.

      iv. **Willful nature of defendant's conduct:** Quite often the defendant's willful or malicious misconduct will make it appropriate to give plaintiff the remedy of her choice.

         (a) **Protection of privacy rights:** Although earlier decisions declined to grant injunctive relief in privacy cases, such reasoning today is rejected outright by practically all courts.

Example: Injunction granted to prevent rejected suitor from continuing to harass plaintiff. [*Kramer v. Douvey*, 680 S.W.2d. 524 (Tex., 1984)].

b. **Test for appropriateness of an injunction.** An injunction is considered appropriate when the remedy at law is inadequate (see above), when the injunction is enforceable, and when the benefit to plaintiff outweighs the hardship to defendant.

    i. **Enforceability of the decree.** Naturally, the court does not want to issue an order that would prove difficult or impossible to enforce. Note that this is generally more of a problem with mandatory injunctions, where the defendant must do an affirmative act that the court must supervise, than with prohibitory injunctions, where the court can simply sanction the defendant for continuing the disallowed activity.

    ii. **Balancing of the hardships.** Where the hardship to the defendant outweighs the benefit of the injunction to the plaintiff, plaintiff's motion for injunction will generally be denied.

    Example: Defendant builds a very expensive boathouse. The boathouse is mostly on his own property, but, after construction is complete, plaintiff discovers that it encroaches 25 feet onto plaintiff's property. When plaintiff brings this to defendant's attention, defendant is horrified, as he did not know that he was encroaching on plaintiff's land. Plaintiff brings a motion for a mandatory injunction ordering defendant to remove the boathouse from his property. Judgment for defendant is likely, as tearing down the boathouse will be considered more of a hardship to defendant than benefit to plaintiff. Note that plaintiff may be able to claim (and win) monetary damages in this situation.

C. NATURE OF INTERESTS PROTECTIBLE IN EQUITY

1. **Unique Chattels:** A mandatory injunction ordering defendant to return a converted chattel is granted where the remedy at law (replevin or damages) is not adequate. To establish the inadequacy of the remedy at law, it must shown that the chattel wrongfully taken is "unique."

a. **Nature of uniqueness:** While uniqueness is variously defined, the underlying principle is that the chattel cannot be replaced through the market. Included within this definition are articles that quite literally are "one of a kind" (e.g., a rare Inca artifact or document signed by George Washington). Also, note that the uniqueness of an item may be based upon *sentimental value* (as in the case of a family heirloom or wedding ring).

Question 1 refers to the following fact pattern.

Deke Deaver hired Sidney Snead, a golf pro, to give lessons to his 14-year-old son, Drake. Deke agreed to pay Sidney $1,000 for ten lessons, which were to be held on Saturday mornings from 10:00 A.M. to 11:00 A.M. When Drake and Deke arrived for the first lesson, they were accompanied by Drake's 6-year-old younger brother, Desmond. As Sidney started his instructional lesson with Drake, Desmond asked if he could participate. Sidney did not object and allowed Desmond to receive instructions along with his brother.

As it turned out, Desmond accompanied Drake and took all ten lessons with his older brother. Each Saturday Deke was present and watched Sidney give the same lessons to both boys. After Desmond and Drake received their last lesson, Sidney requested payment. When Deke presented a check for $1,000, Sidney told Deke that he owed an additional $1,000 for the lessons that Desmond received. After Deke refused to pay for Desmond's lessons, Sidney brought a contract action against Deke for $1,000.

1. Deke will most likely be held liable for

    (A) nothing, because Sidney allowed Desmond to gratuitously participate in the lessons.
    (B) nothing, because no formal contract was entered into between Sidney and Deke.
    (C) $1,000, because an implied-in-fact contract was formed.
    (D) the reasonable value of services rendered, as measured by Desmond's improvement.

Question 2 refers to the following fact pattern.

Crooner was an opera singer who collected rare recordings of opera stars from the 1920s. Collette owned a collection of many old opera recordings that she had inherited from her grandfather. Collette learned of Crooner's interest in rare opera recordings and offered to sell Crooner an opera recording from an obscure tenor, Ralphio, who died after only one recorded performance. Crooner was anxious to obtain the recording because there were no other known copies of a Ralphio recorded performance and it would make Crooner's collection complete. Crooner offered Collette $10,000 for the Ralphio recording subject to certification by Prof. Erickson, a recognized expert in the subject of 20th-century opera singers. Collette wrote to Crooner and accepted the offer. Prior to submitting the recording to Prof. Erickson for certification, Collette received an offer of $20,000 from another collector for the Ralphio recording. Collette told Prof. Erickson that the Ralphio recording was a fake so she could take advantage of the offer from the collector. Prof. Erickson refused to issue the certificate, and Crooner rejected Collette's tender of the recording when she presented it without the certificate.

2. If Crooner discovers the reason why Prof. Erickson would not certify the recording and brings suit against Collette, Crooner may recover

    (A) nothing, because Crooner rejected Collette's tender of the recording.
    (B) money damages only, measured by the difference between the contract and the market price.
    (C) an injunction only, to prevent the sale to the collector.
    (D) specific performance.

Question 3 refers to the following fact pattern.

Player, an experienced antique collector, orally agreed to pay Stringer $250,000 for a rare Stradivarius violin. During their negotiations, both parties referred to the violin as "an original Stradivarius." Stringer, a reputable antique dealer, made no positive representations to that effect, however, and Player relied on his own judgment in the matter. Accordingly, Player paid Stringer $250,000 and received the violin. At the time of the purchase, Stringer also handed Player a "bill of sale" disclaiming, under applicable provisions of the Uniform Commercial Code, all express or implied warranties. The "bill of sale" was signed by Stringer but not by Player.

A short time later, Player discovered that the violin that he purchased was not an original Stradivarius but a masterful imitation. The violin was valued at only $300.

3. Player now brings an appropriate action against Stringer to rescind the contract and recover the $250,000. Which of the following will the court probably decide?

   (A) Stringer will win, because the sales contract was valid and enforceable under the doctrine of caveat emptor.
   (B) Stringer will win, because the "bill of sale" disclaimed any warranties as to the genuineness of the violin.
   (C) Player will win, because although the sales contract was valid, it would be unenforceable under the Statute of Frauds since Player did not sign the "bill of sale."
   (D) Player will win, because although the sales contract was valid, it would be voidable by Player since the parties were mutually mistaken about the genuineness of the violin.

Question 4 refers to the following fact pattern.

Dee Sario had failed the California bar exam three times. On her fourth try, she hired a tutor, Cheri Carney, to help prepare her for the next exam. The parties formalized a written contract in which Cheri promised to tutor Dee for four weeks and Dee promised to pay Cheri $5,000 for her services. At the time the women entered into their agreement, Dee orally promised to pay Cheri an additional $1,000 if she was successful on the bar exam.

4. Assume that Cheri tutored Dee for two weeks when Dee suddenly died from a brain tumor. Cheri made a written demand to Dee's estate seeking payment for services rendered. After the executor of Dee's estate refused to authorize such payment, Cheri filed a contract action against Dee's estate. Cheri should

   (A) recover nothing, because the estate was not unjustly enriched.
   (B) recover nothing, because of impossibility of performance.
   (C) recover quantum meruit, for the reasonable value of services rendered.
   (D) recover $2,500, or the equivalent of one half of the stipulated contract amount.

1.(C)

True contracts are those in which the parties' obligation(s) arise from actual agreement and intent. If the agreement or mutual assent is manifested in words (oral or written), the contract is said to be "express." On the other hand, where the mutual undertaking of the parties is *inferred from their conduct* alone, without spoken or written words, the contract is said to be *"implied in fact."* In this hypo, Deke was present while Desmond received the golf lessons from Snead. Even though the parties did not expressly enter into an agreement with respect to Desmond, it is clear from their conduct that an "implied in fact" contract was created. Note that choice (D) is wrong because it addresses quasi-contractual relief. In a quasi-contract, *the parties do not have a contract and the court constructs one to avoid unjust enrichment.* Here, the parties have entered into a contract by their conduct.

2.(D)

Choice (D) is correct because *specific performance is available to enforce a contract for the sale of a unique item of personal property.* Here, the subject matter of the contract (the Ralphio recording) was the only known recording of its kind. As such, Crooner would be entitled to specific performance of the contract. The condition of certification by Prof. Erickson was excused by Collette's conduct when she falsely told Prof. Erickson that the recording was a fake and thus the failure of the condition to occur would not preclude enforcement of the contract.

3.(D)

It is generally accepted that mutual mistake as to the existence of the subject matter is ground for avoidance of a contract. The difficulty lies in determining what is the subject matter. It may be an object, as where A finds a pretty stone and sells it to B for one dollar, and unknown to both A and B it later turns out to an uncut diamond worth one thousand dollars. A may not rescind and recover the stone. The only mistake was as to the value of the object, not as to its existence. On the other hand, not the object, but its rare quality, may be the subject matter, as where A sells to B a stone for two thousand dollars, both of them thinking it to be a diamond, and it turns out to be a zircon, worth about five dollars. B may rescind and recover the price paid, on the ground of mutual mistake as to the existence of the violin as an "original Stradivarius." Therefore, the contract is voidable by Player.

4.(C)

Ordinarily the death of the offeror terminates the power of acceptance created by a revocable offer. But the situation is different when the death occurs after the formation of the contract. Death does not necessarily discharge a contract. If a contract, however, calls for *personal performance by the promisor and person who is to render the performance dies or becomes ill as to make performance impossible,* the *promisor's duty is excused* unless the risk was assumed. Conversely, we have a situation where the promisee, not the promisor, has died. The *doctrine of frustration of purpose* usually applies in these cases. Moreover, where a contract has been discharged for impossibility or frustration, it is often necessary,

in the interest of justice, to adjust the rights of the parties. In this situation, recovery for part performance should be available. As a result, choice (C) is correct and Cheri will be entitled to recover the reasonable value of services rendered despite the fact that the contract was discharged by frustration.

Note to students: Because Remedies is an interdisciplinary subject, you may encounter essay questions that require you to draw on your knowledge of contract, tort, property, and constitutional law. The same will undoubtedly be true on your law school exams and on the bar exam!

Questions 1 and 2 refer to the following fact pattern.

Al planned to build a large shopping center in a suburban area. Betty agreed in writing to sell Al her 100-acre farm located in the center of the proposed development. Al deposited with Betty a portion of the purchase price, the balance to be paid upon delivery of the deed by Betty. At the time their written contract was entered into, Al told Betty only that he was buying her land and 200 acres from other local farmers for a "big project."

Relying upon Betty's agreement, Al purchased the surrounding 200 acres from other farmers. He paid them the same price he had contracted to pay Betty: $1,000 an acre. This price was $200 an acre over market value.

Claude, hoping to build his own shopping center on other nearby land, paid Betty $100,000 to refuse to convey her property to Al. Betty falsely notified Al that she could not complete the sale because she had discovered a defect in her title. Al reluctantly accepted return of his deposit. Without Betty's land, Al could not develop the shopping center as planned, and he has offered his 200 acres for sale. Claude's shopping center is nearing completion.

Al recently learned of Claude's arrangements with Betty.

What legal and equitable remedies does Al have:

1. Against Betty? Discuss.

2. Against Claude? Discuss.

1. What legal and equitable remedies does Al have against Betty? Discuss.

Al ("A") could sue Betty ("B") for breach of contract ("k"), or fraud.

Breach of contract

With respect to the breach of k action, B could contend that (1) A mutually agreed to rescind the transaction, (2) A suffered no monetary damages, since the $100,000 payment was returned to him, and (3) she could not reasonably foresee that A would lose money with respect to the other parcels of land which he purchased.

In rebuttal, however, A could argue that (1) the agreement to rescind was invalid, since it was procured by a fraud (i.e., B's representation that there was a defect in her title), (2) he did suffer damage by reason of the (i) diminished market value of the other land which he had purchased, and (ii) lost profits with respect to the shopping center, and (3) the losses A has or will incur on the other parcels was reasonably foreseeable, since A had advised B that he was buying 200 acres from other farmers for a "big project." Therefore, B should have recognized that if she withdrew her land (for which A had overpaid), A would be obliged to resell the other land he had purchased.

Based upon the foregoing, A can probably recover in breach of k for the diminished value of the other 200 acres that he purchased but not the lost shopping center profits. The latter are consequential damages, which were likely not foreseeable at the time the contract was entered into and are too speculative (it cannot reasonably be ascertained, had A operated the shopping center, how much profit would have been derived).

Fraud

One is liable in fraud where he deliberately misrepresents a material fact to another, upon which representation the latter justifiably relies to his detriment. Although B would contend that, since A's money was returned to him, there has been no detrimental reliance, this argument should fail (A has suffered losses with respect to the other acres which he purchased).

A would attempt to recover his actual losses to the extent such damages are reasonably susceptible of estimation. Thus, A should be able to recover for the losses suffered as a consequence of the diminished value of the other land he purchased but probably cannot recover for lost shopping center profits because these are too speculative.

A could also contend that a constructive trust in his favor should be imposed upon the $100,000 payment that B received from Claude ("C"). A constructive trust may be imposed where a person acquires property under circumstances where he would be unjustly enriched if permitted to retain it. To permit B to retain the proceeds received from effectuating a fraud upon A (i.e., advising him that she did not have good title to her land) would arguably be inequitable. Thus, A's constructive trust theory could be successful.

Additionally, punitive damages may be recovered for an intentional tort. Such damages seem appropriate in this instance since B's conduct (accepting a bribe to deprive someone of a prospective business advantage) is the type of action that should be discouraged. Note the punitive damages recovery would be based on Betty's act of fraud, not her breach of the contract.

2. **What legal and equitable remedies does Al have against Claude? Discuss.**

A could sue C for intentional interference with a (i) contractual relationship (the outstanding k that A had with B) and, (ii) prospective business advantage (the profits to be made from operation of the shopping center). Since there appears to be no privilege for C's actions, the assertion of these theories should be successful.

With respect to the former action, A could probably recover the difference between the price he paid for the other 200 acres and their present market price. A would, of course, be limited to a single recovery of this amount—be it from B or C. As to the lost profits, however, C could probably contend (as described above) that these damages are too speculative. A could also seek punitive damages for the foregoing intentional torts.

Since monetary damages would not make A whole with respect to the lost opportunity pertaining to the shopping center, he should request that the court issue a temporary restraining order (preventing C from completing and operating the shopping center) until the lawsuit is resolved. A would also request a mandatory injunction, requiring C to transfer his interest in the shopping center to A upon payment to C of his expenses with respect to the site (less any damages for which C is liable to A). It would be feasible to carry out this injunction, since the court could issue an order transferring the shopping center to A if C refused to execute the necessary documents. It is likely that this relief would be granted, since it represents the only means of putting A in the position he would have been in had C not induced B to breach the agreement with A.

NOTES

KAPLAN **pmbr**

NOTES

KAPLAN) *pmbr*

NOTES

KAPLAN) *pmbr*